CHÂTEAU TANUNDA
100 YEAR OLD VINES SHIRAZ
THE SITE OF THE VERY FIRST VINES PLANTED
IN THE BAROSSA VALLEY IN 1845
GRAND BAROSSA
SHIRAZ

PRATO

9 COURSES

9 COURSES

BRANDON McGLAMERY

PHOTOGRAPHY BY MICHAEL PISARRI

Foreword by Anne Quatrano

story farm

WINTER PARK • MIAMI • SANTA BARBARA

9 Courses

Published in the United States by Story Farm, LLC.
www.story-farm.com

Library of Congress Cataloguing-in-Publication Data is available upon request.
ISBN 978-0-983-9053-9-4
Printed in China

Editorial director: Ashley Fraxedas
Book design: David Claytor, Morgan Claytor, Jason Farmand of Hatchet Design
Photo styling: Katie Farmand
Copy editors: Karen Cakebread, Eva Dougherty
Recipe testers: Pam Brandon, Katie Farmand, Minter Byrd, Victoria Allman, Susan Bourgoin
Recipe development: Minter Byrd
Indexing: Heidi Blough
Production management: Tina Dahl

10 9 8 7 6 5 4 3 2 1
First Edition, January 2014

For the two ladies in my life—
Elizabeth, my wife,
and Suzanne, my mom.

And my two little gentlemen,
Ryder and Ashby.

TASTING MENU

FOREWORD

BRANDON McGLAMERY IS ONE OF THE RARE CHEFS who has come through our kitchens; his food is as lovely to the eye as it is on the palate. He has an innate sense of the simple elegance of raw ingredients. We share an affinity for acid (the cooking kind), subtle spice and *Donna Hay Magazine*. I find his food, seasoning and sensibility almost always spot on.

ALL JOKING ASIDE, HIS FOOD OBSESSION NEVER WAVERED, WHICH GARNERED MY FULL RESPECT.

Sounds like a dream chef, eh?

Well, suffice to say that Brandon was barreling through his irreverent 20s at full speed while here in Atlanta. Like most really great chefs, his attention bounced off the walls, focusing only on the dish, the plate, the preparation . . . and whatever was happening in random parking lots behind watering holes late at night. All joking aside, his food obsession never wavered, which garnered my full respect.

9 Courses is a tribute to Brandon's love of Florida, the water, fishing, farming, family and friends. The recipes are thoughtful, with great respect for the wonderful ingredients and those who harvest them. The visuals are a feast for the eyes, and I only wish we lived closer so we could dine at his restaurants frequently.

I am honored to write this foreword and to have had the good fortune of spending time with Brandon in our kitchens. We are so proud of his accomplishments. It really could not have happened to a nicer pain in the ass.

With fond food memories and some others that will remain unmentioned . . .

ANNE QUATRANO
Bacchanalia, Floataway Café, Star Provisions, Quinones, Abattoir
Atlanta, Georgia

INTRODUCTION

THERE'S SOMETHING ABOUT THE NUMBER 9 that I find really appealing.

Maybe it's because I'm an odd kind of guy. Nothing even or symmetrical or in-the-box works for me.

When I was a little kid and just learning how to count, the only way I could keep everything straight was by assigning faces and personalities to numbers. I was drawn to the odd numbers, the even ones not so much. For me, 1 was the brave soldier standing straight at attention, 2 was a scary hunchback, 3 was a fisherman casting out his line, 4 was a threatening figure with a hatchet, and so on.

But 9? Nine was the top of the heap, the end of the line, the coup de grâce. It had stature and authority. For me, 9 was the mother hen watching over her brood before 10 came along, all hell broke loose and everything started repeating itself. Nine brought comfort and a sense of order.

Okay, maybe I was a little whacked out as a kid.

OPPOSITE PAGE
Bay scallops *cottura medie*, recipe on page 46

SO HOW DOES ALL THAT TRANSLATE TO FOOD?

Let's put it this way: if you were to walk into Luma on Park or Prato, sit at one of our chef's tables and say, "Feed me," the food that followed would likely play out in nine thoughtful courses. It would take at least that many dishes for us to tell our story, show you how we cook and help you understand the way we approach food in our restaurants.

Which is not to say you can't drop by, order a single dish and totally enjoy yourself. Quite obviously, not everyone is always up for nine courses at a sitting.

But when I first started thinking about this book and pulling together the recipes and techniques I wanted to include, I approached it as I would a

tasting menu. How do I share the widest possible assortment of my favorite dishes? And how do I pay tribute to the farmers, fishermen, artisanal provisioners—most of them from Florida—who contribute to the way I like to cook?

MANY OF THE DISHES WE CREATE AT OUR RESTAURANTS are the result of what I like to call a food crush. Thanks to our suppliers, our own research or, sometimes, just dumb luck, we get our hands on a great ingredient and fall madly in love with it. Maybe it's shrimp the size of your hand that we source from Andy Duda on Pine Island. Maybe it's strawberries or cranberry beans grown by Denise Muir at Rabbit Run Farm near Fort Myers. Maybe it's the flounder we get from Vince Luise, who goes spearfishing for them off Port Canaveral. Or maybe it's something as simple as a fresh-from-the-hen egg, like those we get from Dale Volkert at Lake Meadow Naturals.

All I know is that once the food crush hits, there's no stopping us. We're obsessed, trying this and experimenting with that, seeing where it takes us. The results aren't always plate-worthy, but every now and then we hit on something where we want to shout, "Taste this!" and share it with the world. That's how many of the dishes in this book evolved, and as I began trying to bring a sense of order to everything, the recipes more or less organized themselves and fell into a natural sequence: Surprises, Raw, Soups, Salads + Eggs, Charcuterie, Pasta, Seafood, Roasts and Sweets.

And thus: *9 Courses*.

AS MUCH AS I WANT THIS BOOK TO BE ROOTED IN THE PRESENT, I suppose a tiny bit of background is in order. So here's the short version.

Grew up in Florida, Naples and Saint Petersburg to be exact. Spent lots of time fishing as a kid, a passion that consumes me as an adult. Worked in kitchens from the age of 15. Dropped out of college and headed to culinary school in California because I heard that was where I'd find all the great chefs. Wound up working with the best of them at that time—Jeremiah Tower, Alice Waters, Craig Stoll and Thomas Keller. Made the de rigueur chef's pilgrimage to Europe so I could worship at the altar of French cuisine. My takeaway was this: our food back home was just as good, if not better, especially in the Bay Area and other big cities. So I vowed to remain in those places that could feed my soul. And I also vowed to never return to Florida to work as a chef because it seemed too much under the influence of giant agribusiness, big chain restaurants and mass production to hold any appeal for serious chefs hoping to forge their own ways.

Which is how I wound up in Atlanta, where the cooking scene was starting to catch fire. At the center of it all was a chef who would become a great mentor and influence, Anne Quatrano of Bacchanalia. She was demanding, yet generous with her knowledge, and we forged the sort of collaboration that I encourage among our chefs in the kitchens of Luma and Prato. It's based on an open exchange of ideas about flavors and the flow of a menu, how one course should set the stage for the next.

Above everything else, Anne taught me this: It's not the brilliance of a chef that makes a memorable dish. Nor is it the technique. Rather, it's all about the ingredients. If you build your dish upon the best ingredients, then creativity and technique will follow. Don't overthink it. Don't try to reinvent the wheel. Let ingredients lead the way.

MEANWHILE, BACK IN THE SUNSHINE State, things were starting to gain speed and get some momentum. Guys like Norman Van Aken were singing the praises of our subtropical abundance and creating Florida-centric dishes long before the whole eat-local thing was cool. What's that saying about how once you have the sand in your shoes you can never really leave Florida? As luck would have it, about the time I started feeling the pull of my boyhood home, I was called back to Florida. I paid a visit to Bob Amick, owner and founder of Atlanta-based Concentrics Restaurants, and Brian France, CEO and chairman of the board of NASCAR. They were getting ready to launch Luma on Park, in Winter Park, and wanted me to take the helm of the kitchen.

I signed on, but didn't really plan on staying for long. I figured I would learn a lot by launching the restaurant, satisfy my longing for Florida and then head off to New York, or maybe back to California, or any number of places where the restaurant scenes were sizzling.

But a few things happened along the way. First and most important, I fell in love, got married and started building a family with my wife, Liz.

Another thing that made me want to stick around: this is where the best ingredients are. In recent years, farmers, fishermen, ranchers and other provisioners have begun to transform Florida into a dream state for those who want to eat local—and to do so year-round. It's always the growing season in Florida. When the rest of the country is just beginning to enjoy locally grown tomatoes, we've had them for months and have already moved on to something else, like fresh peaches or sweet corn, which we get first. Despite all the theme parks and beaches, people sometimes forget that Florida, at its

IT'S ALL ABOUT THE INGREDIENTS. IF YOU BUILD YOUR DISH UPON THE BEST INGREDIENTS, THEN CREATIVITY AND TECHNIQUE WILL FOLLOW.

9 RULES OF THE ROAD

A few quick notes on how to use this book, along with random observations and brilliant insight:

1. **MANY OF THESE RECIPES ARE NOT PAINT-BY-NUMBERS SIMPLE.** Sorry about that, but there's no dumbing down good food. Improvise as necessary. Recipes are roadmaps, but it's OK to wander off the highway. If, say, a recipe calls for mangoes and they suck, use the awesome peaches instead.

2. **DON'T LET THE FOOD BE SMARTER THAN YOU.** It can't think, so it can't win. Never let cooking be a battle.

3. **BUY THE BEST INGREDIENTS YOU CAN AFFORD.** Never compromise on this front. You only live once.

4. **MANY RECIPES SAY, "SEASON TO TASTE."** Yes, this is to *your* best judgment. But keep in mind that you should add just enough salt and pepper so that all the ingredients are allowed to sing on their own.

5. **SALT IS ALWAYS KOSHER,** unless otherwise noted.

6. **HERBS AND SPICES ARE ALWAYS AS FRESH AS HUMANLY POSSIBLE.** And it's worth an extrahuman effort to make sure of that.

7. **BLACK PEPPER IS ALWAYS FRESHLY GROUND OUT OF A PEPPER MILL**—never out of a jar or shaker, which is punishable by death.

8. **COMMON COOKING SENSE TAKES PRECEDENCE** over no sense at all.

9. **HAVE FUN, SMILE OFTEN, EAT WELL.**

And one last thing:
ACID AND SALT ARE KING! BE THE ROADRUNNER!
(I'll explain that later.)

heart, is an agricultural state. A growing network of dedicated farmers offers grass-fed beef, heritage pork and antibiotic-free poultry. And don't even get me started about seafood. From clams and bay scallops to fresh-caught cobia, pompano, red snapper and grouper, it's exciting to see what our fishmongers surprise us with each day.

What finally sealed the deal and made me want to stick around: Winter Park is a great place to live and work. The residents are sophisticated, well traveled and some of the downright friendliest people on this planet. They embody the true sense of community. Those of us who slave away in kitchens feed off our customers, we really do. The more they demand, the more it challenges us. And the more enthusiasm they show, the more it encourages us to push even further. The good people who supported Luma and, later, Prato, especially those who frequented our chef's tables, gave us a platform to interact directly with smart diners and help evolve the concept that became *9 Courses*.

But enough talking about food. It's making me hungry. Let's cut to the first course.

THOSE OF US WHO SLAVE AWAY IN KITCHENS FEED OFF OUR CUSTOMERS, WE REALLY DO.

SURPRISES

FIRST COURSE

We love to kick things off with a surprise, a little bite of something unexpected, in small, jewel box–like presentations that set the stage for good things to come—and leave you hungry for more.

One of my mentors, the great California chef Jeremiah Tower, always liked to say, "The butter should be dripping off your elbows," meaning: excess can be a good thing. Here, we have what amounts to egg on egg on egg—fish eggs atop egg salad atop an egg-luscious brioche. Now that Florida's Mote Marine Laboratory is raising sturgeon commercially, caviar is an amazing local product, not something that comes from halfway around the world. I don't specify the amount of caviar for this recipe; just know that the more you use, the better mood you'll be in and the same goes for anyone who enjoys this dish with you.

CRÈME FRAÎCHE EGG SALAD
WITH CAVIAR AND BUTTER-FRIED BRIOCHE

SERVES 12

CRÈME FRAÎCHE EGG SALAD

4 eggs

Zest of 1 lemon

1 tablespoon shallots, finely diced

2 tablespoons fresh tarragon, finely chopped

2 teaspoons fresh dill, finely chopped

2 tablespoons chives, finely chopped

1 tablespoon Dijon mustard

5 tablespoons crème fraîche

1 teaspoon coarse salt

1 teaspoon freshly ground black pepper

RYE BRIOCHE
Makes a 9-inch loaf

1¾ cups high-gluten flour

¾ cup light rye flour

¼ cup sugar

6 eggs

¼ ounce active dry yeast

1¼ tablespoons kosher salt

1 tablespoon caraway seeds, toasted and finely ground

1½ cups unsalted butter, chilled and cut into small pieces

1 egg yolk

2 tablespoons cream

»

PREPARE EGG SALAD

Place eggs in a small saucepan and cover by 1 inch with cold water. Bring to a simmer and cook for 3 minutes; remove from heat and let eggs stand in hot water, covered, for 7 minutes. Immediately drain and peel eggs under cool water.

Pat eggs dry and press through a fine-mesh strainer, such as a chinois or China cap, into a mixing bowl. Fold in lemon zest, shallots, tarragon, dill, chives, mustard and crème fraîche. Season with salt and pepper. Refrigerate until ready to serve.

PREPARE RYE BRIOCHE

Stir together flours and sugar in a large bowl of an electric mixer.

Bring 2 inches of water to a simmer in a medium saucepan. Whisk together eggs and yeast in a glass bowl and place over simmering water, whisking until mixture is warm to the touch.

Add warm egg mixture to flour mixture. Using an electric mixer fitted with the paddle attachment, beat on medium speed until dough comes together in a ball. With machine running, slowly add salt and caraway seeds. Continue to mix, quickly adding butter piece by piece. Mix until dough is shiny and makes a slapping sound on sides of bowl, about 6 minutes.

Remove dough from bowl, tighten into a ball, and place in a large buttered bowl. Cover with plastic wrap and allow dough to rise at room temperature for about 2 hours. Gently lift sides of dough and fold back toward center. Refrigerate overnight.

Butter and flour a 9-inch pullman loaf pan. Place dough in pan, cover with plastic wrap and let rise at room temperature until dough nearly reaches rim of pan.

Preheat oven to 375°F. Whisk together egg yolk and cream; gently brush top of loaf and bake for 20 minutes. Remove from oven, cover with foil, and continue to bake for 20 to 25 minutes more or until golden brown.

Cool in pan on rack for 10 minutes. Turn out loaf onto rack; cool at least 1 hour.

ASSEMBLE

Slice bread into 1-inch-thick slices. Remove crusts and cut each slice into 4 smaller squares.

Melt 2 tablespoons butter in a large skillet over medium heat until slightly foamy. Add bread squares, lightly coating both sides with melted butter. Toast in pan, turning until both sides are golden. Repeat with remaining squares, adding more butter as needed.

Top each toasted square with egg salad and garnish with caviar and chervil.

FOR ASSEMBLY

Butter for toasting brioche

Caviar (as much as you can possibly afford)

Chervil, for garnish

Truffled popcorn is by far the most popular dish at Luma, and it's not even on the menu. Its origins go back to when I was a boy and visiting my Aunt Adrienne and Uncle Gary. Uncle Gary worked in the restaurant business, and when he came home late in the evening he would pop himself a big bowl of popcorn and then, to finish it off, reach for the green can of Parmesan (or what we thought was Parmesan back then). I fell in love with the flavor, and creating variations on Uncle Gary's popcorn—curry, Tabasco, bacon—was my first foray into playing around with food. We use plain microwave popcorn because it allows us to add oils without oversaturating with fat. If you feel like splurging, use fresh shaved truffles. It's your call. And your wallet.

TRUFFLED POPCORN

MAKES ABOUT 6 CUPS

1 bag plain microwave popcorn (or ⅓ cup regular unpopped popcorn)

1 ounce Parmigiano-Reggiano cheese, finely grated (about ¾ cup)

1 tablespoon white truffle oil

1 tablespoon extra-virgin olive oil

½ teaspoon black truffle salt or kosher salt

3 tablespoons chives, thinly sliced

OPTIONAL GARNISHES

Parmigiano-Reggiano cheese, shaved

White or black truffles, freshly shaved

Prepare popcorn according to package directions and, while still warm, toss with Parmesan, followed by both oils, salt and chives.

This is our twist on the oyster shooter, a celebratory canapé that's a fun way to start any meal. We love to use Florida oysters in the cooler months, but cold-water oysters will do the trick year-round, too. The sangrita works as a kind of deconstructed cocktail sauce, and you can amp up the heat to suit your taste, or go heavier with the tequila if it suits your style.

APALACHICOLA OYSTERS
IN SANGRITA CONSOMMÉ

MAKES 16

SANGRITA CONSOMMÉ

(Prepare at least 6 hours before serving)

2 pounds red tomatoes, quartered

1 large cucumber, peeled and seeded

1 jalapeño, halved and seeded

½ cup chopped red onion

½ cup tangerine juice

½ cup lime juice

1 tablespoon agave nectar (can substitute honey or simple syrup)

2 tablespoons Worcestershire sauce

2 tablespoons Tabasco sauce

1 tablespoon kosher salt

1 teaspoon Jerry Garcia Spice Blend (page 216)

Reserved oyster juice, strained

OYSTERS

16 Apalachicola oysters, shucked, juices reserved

FOR ASSEMBLY

½ cup tequila blanco, top shelf, well chilled

16 lime slices

PREPARE CONSOMMÉ

Place all ingredients in a blender or food processor and puree until smooth. Adjust seasonings to taste. Line a sieve or colander with cheesecloth and let mixture strain through it in refrigerator for at least 6 hours, or overnight.

PREPARE OYSTERS

Bring 4 cups of lightly salted water to a simmer. Lower 8 oysters into the water for 20 seconds and then transfer them to an ice water bath. Repeat process with remaining oysters. Drain and chill until ready to assemble.

ASSEMBLE

Make sure consommé and tequila are well chilled. Mix together and half-fill 16 chilled shot glasses with mixture. Add 1 oyster to each and then continue filling glasses to the rim with consommé-tequila mixture. Garnish with lime slices.

Sous chef Mike Tully and I came up with this after *Playboy* magazine called to ask if we could contribute a "croquette" recipe. We didn't want to use mashed potatoes, as is typical for croquettes, so we turned it into an homage to a Spanish tapas mainstay and a favorite at Cuban takeout windows in Miami's Little Havana. You can use lobster or chicken instead of shrimp; just make sure the batter is extracold before shaping the croquetas. This is one of my favorite snacks because there is so much going on—hot, cool, creamy, spicy. They loved it at *Playboy*, but I'm still waiting for my invitation to Hef's mansion.

PINE ISLAND SHRIMP CROQUETAS

SERVES 8

CROQUETAS

4 tablespoons (½ stick) unsalted butter

1 teaspoon Espelette pepper

1 medium spring onion, finely chopped (about 1 cup)

1¼ cups all-purpose flour, sifted, plus 1 cup

2 cups whole milk

1 tablespoon kosher salt

10 ounces Pine Island shrimp, cooked, finely chopped, and chilled

2 cups finely grated Manchego cheese, loosely packed

2 tablespoons parsley, finely chopped

2 large eggs, beaten

1 cup panko "fino"

4 cups canola, grapeseed or vegetable oil

CUCUMBER-JALAPEÑO GAZPACHO

1 small spring onion, sliced paper-thin (about ½ cup)

2 tablespoons lime juice

2 tablespoons white wine vinegar

1½ teaspoons kosher salt

2 large cucumbers, peeled and seeded

1 jalapeño, roasted, peeled and seeded

1 garlic clove

PREPARE CROQUETAS

Melt butter in a large saucepan and add pepper and onion. Slowly sweat onion until soft. Sprinkle sifted flour over onion and mix well. Cook over low heat for 5 minutes. Slowly add milk while whisking vigorously to avoid lumps. Add salt and continue cooking, stirring occasionally, until sauce has thickened. Transfer to a mixing bowl.

After sauce has cooled slightly, fold in shrimp, cheese and parsley. Season with salt to taste and refrigerate until well chilled.

When batter is extremely cold, scoop scant 2-tablespoon measures and form into 16 oblong croquetas. Place on a parchment-lined sheet pan and chill until ready to fry.

PREPARE GAZPACHO

Combine onion, lime juice, vinegar and salt. Let mixture rest for 30 minutes. Strain, lightly squeezing liquid from onions, and reserve liquid. Place cucumbers, jalapeño, onion and garlic into the bowl of a food processor and puree until smooth. Adjust seasoning with reserved lime-vinegar liquid and salt. Refrigerate until ready to serve.

FINISH CROQUETAS

Pour oil into a heavy skillet and heat to 350°F.

Place remaining flour, the eggs and panko in three separate, shallow bowls. Working with just a few of the chilled croquetas at a time, quickly and gently roll each in flour, dip in egg and roll in panko. Drop in heated oil and fry until golden brown. Drain on paper towels and season with salt. Repeat process with remaining chilled croquetas.

ASSEMBLE

Divide gazpacho among 8 small bowls and top each portion with 2 croquetas.

PINE ISLAND SHRIMP

PEOPLE OFTEN TURN UP THEIR NOSES at the idea of using farm-raised fish. It conjures images of artificial colorants, antibiotics, pesticides, preservatives and all those other things we want to keep away from our food.

I had my doubts, too, until I crossed paths with Andy Duda, who raises spectacular shrimp—bigger than the palm of your hand, with a sweet, wild flavor—at his aquaculture operation on Pine Island, just south of Charlotte Harbor. And he does it by following the best possible practices that we look for in any supplier or farmer: sustainable feed sources, minimal environmental impact, a closed pond system with recycled water, low stocking densities and no genetic modification of any kind.

While the science behind Duda's shrimp farm is cutting edge, the day-to-day operation is decidedly low-tech.

"It's just me and my cast net," says Duda, who can haul in 10 or 12 dozen shrimp with a good throw. "This operation is just about as low-impact as you can get."

So when you see Pine Island shrimp in one of our dishes—we use it in all kinds of ways, every chance we get—know that it's not just some convenient name we dreamed up for the sake of local credibility. It's shrimp from right here in Florida, harvested by a guy who cares deeply about what he does.

Here in Florida we can get fresh squash blossoms pretty much year-round, so we like to experiment by stuffing them with all sorts of things, including stone crab and lobster. This variation reunites the blossom with the squash to create a dish that tastes like summer.

FRIED SQUASH BLOSSOMS
WITH ZUCCHINI PUTTANESCA FRESCA

MAKES 8

SQUASH BLOSSOMS

2 cups ricotta cheese, hung overnight in cheesecloth

½ cup finely grated pecorino cheese

Zest of 1 lemon

1 tablespoon fines herbes (assorted herb mixture, such as chives, dill, chervil and basil)

Kosher salt

8 large squash blossoms, freshly picked

8 cups grapeseed or canola oil

BATTER

1 cup all-purpose flour

½ cup semolina flour

1 teaspoon kosher salt

1–1½ cups sparkling water, very cold

ZUCCHINI PUTTANESCA FRESCA

5 medium zucchini, julienned (about 8 cups)

2 cups cherry tomatoes, halved

8 white anchovies, halved

¼ cup chopped capers

¼ cup chopped Italian parsley

½ cup white balsamic vinegar

½ cup extra-virgin olive oil

PREPARE SQUASH BLOSSOMS

In a medium bowl, mix ricotta, pecorino, lemon zest and fines herbes. Season to taste and place mixture in a piping bag with a ½-inch hole. Fill center cavity of each blossom with cheese mixture, leaving petal tips free of cheese. Do not overfill. Gently twist ends of petals to seal. Cover with a damp cloth and refrigerate until well chilled.

PREPARE BATTER

Combine flours and salt in a medium mixing bowl placed over a second bowl filled with ice. Whisk in just enough sparkling water to make a loose batter that pours off a spoon but is not too runny or thin.

PREPARE ZUCCHINI SALAD

Place all ingredients in a medium bowl and mix well. Season to taste with salt.

FINISH BLOSSOMS

Pour oil into a heavy pot and heat to 375°F, using a deep-fry thermometer.

Working in batches, dip blossoms in batter and gently drop into oil. Fry for 1 to 2 minutes, until lightly browned. Drain on paper towels and season with salt. Repeat process with remaining chilled blossoms.

ASSEMBLE

Divide zucchini salad among 8 plates and top with a squash blossom.

This is a trip to Spain with a Florida twist. A classic brandade features salt cod and olive oil, but we've upped the ante with two of our local seafood favorites. I grew up catching grouper and gathering spiny lobsters in Florida, and this is a special combination of two things I remember fondly from my boyhood. This dish is a great way to start a meal and makes people hungry for what comes next.

SPINY LOBSTER AND GROUPER BRANDADE FRITTERS WITH CHORIZO AIOLI

MAKES 16

CHORIZO OIL

(Must be made a day in advance)

2 ounces shallot (about 1 large), thinly sliced

1 ounce garlic (about 3 cloves), peeled and halved

8 ounces dried chorizo, diced

¼ cup tomato paste

1 bay leaf

1 teaspoon spicy smoked pimentón (Spanish paprika)

1 tablespoon sweet smoked pimentón

2⅔ cups grapeseed oil

CHORIZO AIOLI

2 egg yolks

1 tablespoon Dijon mustard

1¼ cups Chorizo Oil, room temperature

1 tablespoon lemon juice

1 tablespoon water

Kosher salt

PREPARE CHORIZO OIL

Lightly sweat shallot and garlic for a couple of minutes over medium-high heat. Add chorizo, and increase heat slightly to let chorizo release its fat. Cook for about 10 minutes.

Add tomato paste, bay leaf and both pimentóns. Cook until very fragrant, stirring frequently so mixture does not stick.

Add oil and bring to a simmer. Remove from heat, place in a sealed container and refrigerate overnight.

The next day, put chorizo oil in a saucepot and return to simmer. Cook for 2 minutes and strain though a fine strainer. Chill oil until ready to use, discarding the chorizo sediment.

PREPARE CHORIZO AIOLI

Place egg yolks and mustard in the bowl of a food processor. With the machine running, slowly drizzle in chorizo oil. Add lemon juice and water and season to taste.

»

LOBSTER AND GROUPER FRITTERS

1 pound grouper fillet, diced into ½-inch cubes

½ pound spiny lobster, diced small

Kosher salt

2 cups heavy cream

1 sprig rosemary

1 bay leaf

10 black peppercorns

4 garlic cloves, Microplaned

10 ounces Yukon gold potatoes (about 2 medium), cooked, peeled, riced and kept warm

Freshly ground black pepper

4 cups canola oil

1 cup all-purpose flour

2 large eggs, beaten

1 cup panko "fino"

PREPARE FRITTERS

Keeping them separate, season grouper and lobster liberally with salt. Let rest for 30 minutes. Rinse and pat dry.

Place cream, rosemary, bay leaf, peppercorns and garlic in a small saucepot and bring to a simmer over medium-high heat. Cook for 2 minutes. Strain cream mixture through a fine-mesh sieve into a larger saucepot, discarding the solids.

Over very low heat, add grouper to cream mixture and gently cook through, about 2 minutes. With a slotted spoon, remove grouper and place in a mixing bowl. Repeat the same process for lobster. Add lobster to grouper when finished, reserving cream.

Using a mixer fitted with the paddle attachment, mix grouper and lobster for 1 minute on medium speed to break up slightly. Add warm potatoes and mix with ¼ cup plus 1 tablespoon reserved cooking cream. Season to taste.

Shape mixture into 16 tube-shaped fritter portions, each about 2 inches long, and chill until ready to fry.

Heat canola oil in a saucepot (or deep fryer) over medium-high heat until it reaches 350°F. Roll fritters in flour, then dip in egg, then roll in panko. Fry in small batches for 2 minutes per side or until golden brown. Let rest on paper towels while cooking remaining fritters, allowing the oil to return to 350°F between batches.

ASSEMBLE

Place 2 fritters on each plate with 1 tablespoon chorizo aioli between them.

With Florida growers embracing a wider selection of tropical fruits, it's easier to source things like passion fruit, one of our favorite ingredients. Although *uni* (sea urchin roe) is not common in Florida, we love to use it whenever we can get our hands on it. You can easily substitute crab or shrimp for uni in this dish.

UNI WITH PASSION FRUIT, COCONUT MILK AND SERRANO

MAKES 8

COCONUT MILK EMULSION

- 1 (13.5-ounce) can coconut milk, unsweetened
- 2 serrano peppers, split lengthwise
- 3 tablespoons grated ginger
- 4 tablespoons diced lemongrass
- 1 tablespoon fish sauce
- 3 tablespoons sugar
- 2 tablespoons lime juice
- 3 lemon basil sprigs
- 3 mint sprigs

UNI

- 8 uni portions, 1 to 2 ounces each

FOR ASSEMBLY

- 4 passion fruits
- ½ cup Coconut Milk Emulsion
- 8 small cilantro leaves or microgreens
- 8 paper-thin serrano pepper slices, soaked in ice water for 30 minutes
- Rock salt, to line platter (can be mixed with various spices as you please)

PREPARE COCONUT MILK EMULSION

Place first 6 ingredients in a medium saucepan and bring to a simmer. Remove from heat and add lime juice, basil and mint. Let steep for 30 minutes. Strain mixture into a small bowl and chill.

PREPARE PASSION FRUIT

Cut each passion fruit in half crosswise. Scoop out the pulp and seeds into a small bowl. Reserve the cleanly scraped fruit halves to use as serving cups. Using a fork, free the pulp and seeds from the sacs. Discard sacs.

ASSEMBLE

Place equal portions of passion fruit in reserved fruit halves. Add 1 tablespoon coconut emulsion and top with a piece of uni. Garnish with a cilantro leaf and a serrano slice. Nest the passion fruit cups on a platter filled with rock salt.

RAW

SECOND COURSE

OK, not *all* the dishes in this chapter are raw. Some are marinated and others are just barely cooked. But I've always been fascinated with Japanese minimalism in the preparation of fish and proteins, and this is where we have fun playing off the combinations of hot and cold, spicy and sweet, soft and crunchy. Over the years, these dishes have been some of our favorites, since they often draw in non-adventurous diners who might not otherwise wander far from the straight and narrow.

For success in each of these dishes, I cannot emphasize enough how the ingredients need to be first-rate and as fresh as possible.

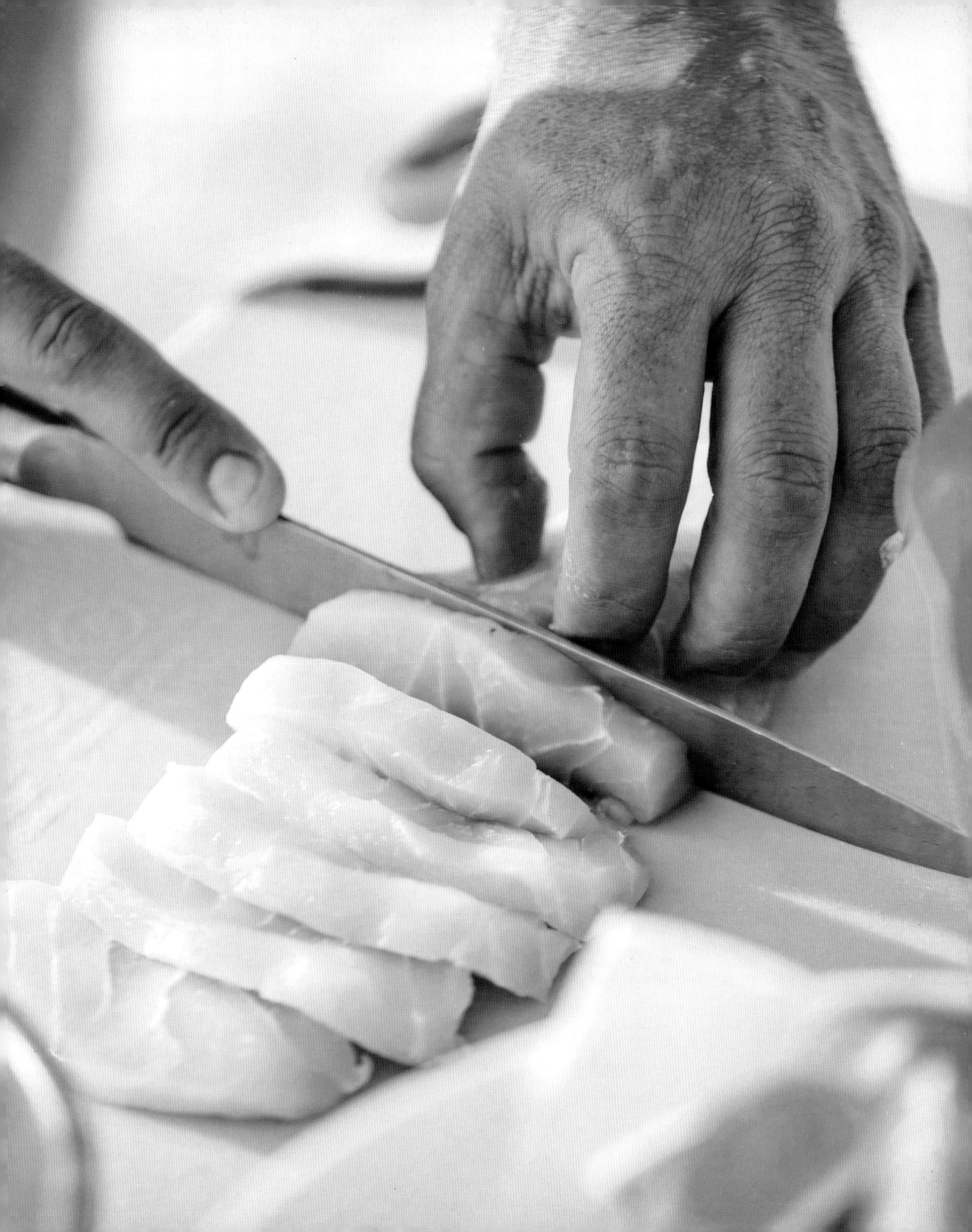

Wahoo is a favorite offshore game fish from Florida waters, and if you can get your hands on some superfresh fillets, you will be stoked by its deep flavor and fatty texture. The watermelon here is compressed with a little vanilla simple syrup and then finished with a vanilla salt, a technique I learned from one of my mentors, Anne Quatrano, of Bacchanalia in Atlanta. This dish is vintage A.Q.: bold, stylish, full of fresh premium produce and simple, but with a distinct feminine flair.

WAHOO SASHIMI SALAD

WITH PLUM, WATERMELON, TOMATOES AND VANILLA SALT

SERVES 8

WATERMELON WATER
(Must be made a day in advance)

½ pound fresh seedless watermelon pulp

¼ pound vine-ripe tomatoes

1 red jalapeño

2 garlic cloves

6 basil leaves

2 tablespoons kosher salt

1 cup sparkling water

VANILLA SIMPLE SYRUP
(Must be made a day in advance)

1 vanilla bean, split and scraped

2 cups sugar

2 cups water

VANILLA SALT

½ cup Maldon sea salt

½ vanilla bean, split and scraped

WAHOO SASHIMI SALAD

1 (5- to 7-pound) seedless red watermelon *(must be compressed a day in advance)*

1½ pounds wahoo, thinly sliced (about 40–50 slices)

Juice of 2 limes

2 cups heirloom cherry tomatoes, halved

1 plum, thinly sliced

2–4 red or yellow serrano peppers, sliced and soaked in ice water

Kosher salt

FOR ASSEMBLY

24 basil leaves or flowers

½ cup extra-virgin olive oil

PREPARE COMPRESSED WATERMELON

(Note: If you don't have a Cryovac machine and prefer not to go to the trouble of compressing, it's fine to use serving-bowl-size pieces of watermelon.)

Cut off the sides and ends of the watermelon and continue cutting away the rind, squaring the pulp until it's the size of a brick. Save excess pulp for the watermelon water.

Compress watermelon brick in a Cryovac machine with ½ cup vanilla simple syrup (procedure below). Keep chilled for up to 24 hours.

PREPARE WATERMELON WATER

Place all ingredients in a blender and puree until smooth. Strain through a cheesecloth into a container and refrigerate overnight. The next day, strain again through a coffee filter to obtain a clear juice.

PREPARE VANILLA SYRUP

Place the vanilla bean scrapings (with seeds), sugar, and water in a saucepot and bring to a boil. Remove and chill in refrigerator. Keeps almost forever.

NOTE The vanilla simple syrup also tastes great in mint iced tea.

PREPARE VANILLA SALT

Scrape the seeds into the salt with the pod and place in a warm spot overnight to dry out the vanilla. Mix well and put into a sealed container. Keeps for even longer than the vanilla simple syrup.

PREPARE SASHIMI SALAD

In a large bowl, toss the wahoo slices, lime juice, cherry tomatoes, plum, and peppers. Season to taste.

ASSEMBLE

Slice compressed watermelon into 8 flat pieces and place 1 piece in each bowl, trimming to fit if necessary. Artfully arrange the salad on top of the watermelon slices.

Garnish with basil, and pour ½ cup watermelon water into each bowl. Top with vanilla salt and drizzle with olive oil.

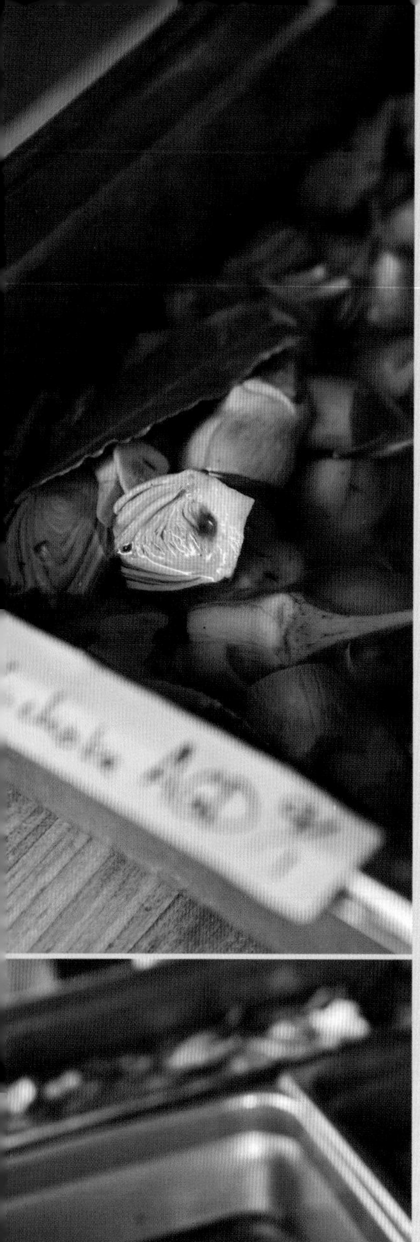

PICKLING THINGS

I HAVE ALWAYS BEEN A BIG FAN OF SWEET AND SOUR. As a kid, I found the condiment shelf to be the most interesting place in our home refrigerator, with everything from marmalades to mustards to crunchy vinegar-laden cucumbers. To this day, when I am snooping around someone else's home refrigerator, that's where I look first to size them up.

We often find ourselves with a surplus of produce grown by our local farmers. They put so much hard work into what they do that we hate wasting anything they send us. That's where pickling comes in. There's a good reason why pickling has long been an American tradition. It's easy. It allows us to enjoy certain veggies when they are long out of season. And the tangy results add a special pop to whatever dish in which you use them.

We have a variety of methods that we use to achieve our end results: blanching the vegetables in pickling liquid until cooked though (agrodolce) and then slipping into an herb-infused olive oil; pouring the hot pickling liquid over an ingredient to retain its crunch and natural state (quick pickle); cooking veggies in a hot oil, removing from heat and hitting with the vinegar (à la grecque); or the traditional pickling in sealed jars.

Experiment with your pickling mediums. For basic purposes, we use white vinegar with light-colored vegetables (cauliflower, fennel) and red vinegar with dark vegetables (beets, okra). You can also play around with spices and herbs. We like thyme, bay leaves, fennel, cardomom and coriander. And the best results come from using them in a sachet.

- Always start with superfresh produce and clean hands.
- Make sure your jars have been sterilized in boiling water or in the dishwasher.
- Fill jars with vegetables first.
- Fill jars with pickling mixture to about ¼ inch from top, keeping rims clean.

- Take a wooden spoon handle and press vegetables toward the sides of the jars to release all air bubbles. Make sure the jar rim is clean and dry, then top with lids and rings and hand tighten.
- Place jars on a rack in a hot water bath with the water halfway up the sides. Keep the water at medium heat and process for about 15 minutes, allowing the lids to push up from the pressure of the escaping air. The lids should no longer flex when you push down on them.
- Roll jars onto their sides to submerge fully for about a minute, releasing the last bits of air to fully seal.
- Transfer jars to a rack and let cool overnight to room temperature. The lids should pull down and seal.
- When in doubt, turn to another solid source as we often do, like *The Joy of Pickling* by Linda Ziedrich.

THERE'S A GOOD REASON WHY PICKLING HAS LONG BEEN AN AMERICAN TRADITION. IT'S EASY.

NOTE You can find several of our pickling recipes in Pantry, beginning on page 212.

I love Thai flavors, and we always keep Thai basil flowers around the kitchen to use as a garnish. Here, we cure the snapper with sugar, salt and citrus juices, creating a sand that cakes and gently cooks the fish. You'll need to make the sorbet at least a day before you serve this dish. But it's worth the effort because the sorbet plays against the salty cashew butter and the mango, giving every mouthful a memorable pop.

RED SNAPPER CEVICHE

WITH CASHEW BUTTER, PICKLED MANGO AND JALAPEÑO SORBET

SERVES 8

JALAPEÑO SORBET

3 jalapeños

2 cups water

¾ cup glucose syrup

2 teaspoons kosher salt

2 tablespoons freshly squeezed lime juice, strained

PICKLED MANGO

¼ cup rice wine vinegar

¼ teaspoon sugar

¼ teaspoon salt

½ cup mango, diced ¼ inch

CASHEW BUTTER

6 ounces roasted and salted cashews

1 teaspoon kosher salt

3 ounces extra-virgin olive oil

RED SNAPPER

1 pound red snapper fillets, skin and blood line removed

2 cups kosher salt

1 cup fine sugar

Zest and juice of 3 oranges

Zest and juice of 3 limes

FOR ASSEMBLY

¼ cup cashew pieces, lightly toasted

8 lime supremes, cut crosswise into thin triangles

¼ cup Thai basil flowers and small leaves

16 to 24 thin jalapeño slices, soaked in ice water for 1 hour

2 tablespoons extra-virgin olive oil

PREPARE SORBET

Slice 2 jalapeños in half lengthwise and remove seeds and membranes. Slice third jalapeño in half lengthwise but retain seeds and membranes to provide a little heat to the sorbet.

Place jalapeños and remaining ingredients in a medium saucepan and bring to a simmer. Stir mixture, making sure syrup and salt dissolve. Transfer to a container and refrigerate overnight.

The following day, strain mixture and process in an ice cream maker until thickened. Freeze until ready to use.

PREPARE PICKLED MANGO

Place vinegar, sugar and salt in a small saucepan and bring to a simmer. Pour over mango and refrigerate for at least 30 minutes. (Can be prepared up to 24 hours in advance.) Drain prior to use.

PREPARE CASHEW BUTTER

Grind cashews and salt in a food processor while streaming in oil. Transfer to a container and refrigerate until ready to use.

PREPARE SNAPPER

Combine salt, sugar, zest and juice to make a wet "sand" and cover snapper on all sides. Refrigerate for 20 to 30 minutes and then rinse. Dry with paper towels and slice thinly at a slight angle.

ASSEMBLE

Swirl 1 tablespoon cashew butter on bottom of 8 individual serving bowls. Evenly distribute half the cashew pieces and half the mango on top.

Arrange equal portions of snapper in center of each bowl and garnish with remaining cashews, mango and lime triangles. Scatter basil flowers and leaves and jalapeño slices over snapper and drizzle with olive oil. Top with small scoop of jalapeño sorbet.

Grouper isn't often served raw in Florida, but it should be. For this dish, we prefer Atlantic grouper from deep water. We like it best in colder months when fresh cranberries are available. Here, the grouper is thinly sliced but not pounded. And the raw kohlrabi gives it just the right crunch.

BLACK GROUPER CARPACCIO WITH CRANBERRY WATER, TAPENADE AND KOHLRABI SALAD

SERVES 8

CRANBERRY WATER

½ cup cold water

½ cup sugar

½ small jalapeño

2½ cups fresh cranberries

1¼ cups San Pellegrino water

8 fresh basil leaves

TAPENADE

¼ cup kalamata olives, pitted

½ garlic clove, Microplaned

½ white anchovy

¼ cup extra-virgin olive oil

KOHLRABI SALAD

1 kohlrabi

1 cup frisée, white part only, torn by hand into fine pieces

20 supersmall fresh mint leaves

Pinch of coarse salt

1 tablespoon extra-virgin olive oil, or to taste

GROUPER

2 pounds black grouper, very thinly sliced

FOR ASSEMBLY

½ cup extra-virgin olive oil

56 thin slices fresh cranberry

PREPARE CRANBERRY WATER

Stir together water, sugar and jalapeño in a medium saucepan over medium heat. Bring to a boil, reduce heat and simmer for 5 minutes. Remove from heat and steep until cooled to room temperature. Strain and set aside.

Once cooled, puree the syrup, cranberries, San Pellegrino and basil in a blender until smooth. Suspend 4 layers of cheesecloth over a glass pitcher or bowl; pour the puree into the cheesecloth to strain the juice. Refrigerate for 8 to 10 hours. Do not squeeze to extract more liquid.

PREPARE TAPENADE

In the small bowl of a food processor, puree ingredients to make a smooth paste. Refrigerate until ready to use. Can be made ahead of time.

PREPARE KOHLRABI SALAD

Peel and square kohlrabi. Thinly slice with a mandoline, then julienne.

Place kohlrabi, frisée and mint in a mixing bowl. Add salt and olive oil; lightly toss.

ASSEMBLE

Arrange fish slices in a circular fashion without overlapping in 8 serving bowls. Drizzle each with 2 tablespoons cranberry water.

Dot grouper with tapenade, then arrange salad in middle of each plate, drizzling fish with 1 tablespoon olive oil. Place 7 slices of cranberry around each plate.

One of my favorite childhood memories is going out on the Homosassa River with my father and brother to gather scallops. My father knew it was a great way to wear us out and provide him with dinner. He had a little stove on his boat and we would sauté our harvest in garlic butter. Often was the day when all the scallops were gone before we got back to shore.

Cottura medie roughly means "barely cooked" in Italian. You can use any kind of bay scallops for this dish, but we prefer the extrasweet ones from Nantucket, especially when the scallop season is closed in Florida. Poaching them for just a few seconds and then shocking them in a cold container of the poaching liquid keeps them almost raw and preserves that briny scallop flavor. We use this same versatile poaching liquid for everything from shrimp and crab to yellowfin tuna.

BAY SCALLOPS COTTURA MEDIE

WITH CRISPY SUNCHOKES, POPPY SEEDS AND POMEGRANATE-GRAPEFRUIT VINEGAR

SERVES 8

SCALLOPS

- 8⅓ cups water
- 1 (750-ml) bottle dry white wine
- 2 jalapeños, sliced
- ¼ cup sugar
- ½ cup kosher salt
- ¼ cup coriander seeds
- ¼ cup fennel seeds
- ¼ pound fresh basil
- 1 pound Nantucket bay scallops, cleaned

POMEGRANATE-GRAPEFRUIT VINEGAR

- 4 tablespoons minced shallot
- ¼ cup red wine vinegar
- Kosher salt
- 2 tablespoons freshly squeezed Ruby Red grapefruit juice
- 2 tablespoons pomegranate juice, freshly squeezed if possible

PREPARE SCALLOPS

Combine water, wine, jalapeños, sugar and salt in a large pot. Bring to a simmer.

Meanwhile, toast coriander and fennel seeds in a small skillet over medium heat, stirring constantly, until fragrant and golden brown in spots. Immediately place in the simmering liquid.

Remove pot from heat and add basil. Let steep for 30 minutes, then strain. Refrigerate until ready to use.

Bring half of poaching liquid to a simmer in a large saucepan. Place the other half in a medium bowl set inside an ice bath; keep well chilled.

In 3 or 4 batches (so temperature of poaching liquid doesn't drop too rapidly when scallops are added), poach the scallops in the simmering broth for 15 seconds. Immediately transfer to cold broth to stop the cooking.

Reserve in cold poaching liquid for a minimum of 30 minutes and up to 24 hours, then dry before plating.

PREPARE VINEGAR

Place shallot in a medium bowl; cover with vinegar and add a pinch of salt. Let sit 30 minutes, then stir in grapefruit and pomegranate juices. Refrigerate for at least 30 minutes.

PREPARE SUNCHOKES

Pour oil into a large pot to a depth of 1 inch. Heat to 350°F.

Working in batches, fry sunchokes until golden brown, 2 to 3 minutes. Drain on paper towels. Season to taste while still warm.

ASSEMBLE

Toss drained poached scallops with a drizzle of oil, some grapefruit segments, pomegranate seeds and radish slices. Season to taste with salt.

Evenly divide mixture among 4 to 8 serving bowls. Garnish each serving with a sprinkle of poppy seeds and a few radish sprouts. Top with sunchokes.

CRISPY SUNCHOKES

Vegetable oil

1 pound fresh sunchokes (Jerusalem artichokes), scrubbed thinly sliced and patted dry

Kosher salt

FOR ASSEMBLY

Extra-virgin olive oil

16 to 24 grapefruit segments

½ cup fresh pomegranate seeds

2 to 4 large radishes, shaved

Kosher salt

1 tablespoon poppy seeds

Radish sprouts

I learned how to cook the classic tuna paillard from chef Jeremiah Tower at Stars restaurant in San Francisco, and this is our twist on it. The name comes from the fact that, like a fried egg, one side of the tuna is cooked and the other is not. Topping the tuna with a slightly warm vinaigrette makes for a nice contrast with the chill of the undercooked fish.

YELLOWFIN TUNA "SUNNY-SIDE UP"

WITH OYSTER MUSHROOMS AND ASPARAGUS

SERVES 8

SHERRY VINAIGRETTE

2 tablespoons minced shallots

2 tablespoons Dijon mustard

⅓ cup Xérès sherry vinegar

1¼ cups extra-virgin olive oil

Kosher salt and freshly ground black pepper

GARLIC BREAD CRUMBS

½ loaf ciabatta or sourdough bread, crusts removed

¼ cup extra-virgin olive oil

1 garlic clove, finely grated

Kosher salt

OYSTER MUSHROOMS

2 tablespoons grapeseed oil

1 pound oyster mushrooms

2 garlic cloves, very thinly sliced

1 cup Sherry Vinaigrette

8 asparagus spears, thinly sliced on diagonal and blanched

1 cup English peas, blanched

½ cup thinly sliced chives

TUNA

1½ pounds yellowfin tuna, cut into 8 (½-inch-thick) steaks (about 3 ounces each)

Kosher salt and freshly ground black pepper

Maldon sea salt for garnish

PREPARE VINAIGRETTE

Place shallots and mustard in a medium bowl and add vinegar. Mix well and allow to macerate for 20 minutes. Whisk in oil and season to taste.

PREPARE BREAD CRUMBS

Preheat oven to 250°F. Tear bread into small pieces and heat in oven until completely dry but without coloring, about 20 minutes.

Place dried bread in a food processor and pulse to uniform-size crumbs. Heat oil in a large sauté pan over medium heat. Toast the crumbs, stirring constantly, until a light golden brown. Lower the heat, add garlic and continue stirring another minute or two. Place on a plate to cool and season with salt.

PREPARE MUSHROOMS

Place oil in a large sauté pan over medium-high heat. Add mushrooms and pan roast until lightly caramelized. Lower heat and add garlic. When garlic begins to soften, mix in vinaigrette and slowly heat. Add asparagus, peas and chives and gently warm. Season to taste.

PREPARE TUNA

Heat a large, well-seasoned frying pan over high heat. Working in batches, quickly sear each steak on one side only. Place each steak, seared side down, on a warmed plate and season to taste. Top each with mushrooms, 1 tablespoon garlic bread crumbs and Maldon salt.

When cobia are running in Florida, we just can't get enough of this tasty white-fleshed fish. But it's easy to overcook cobia, and here we give it just a brief poach in an extra-virgin olive oil marinade so it's only a step away from raw. The granita starts to melt the moment it hits the fish, creating a tangy chilled sauce and a nice texture contrast.

COBIA POACHED IN OLIVE OIL, WITH JICAMA, AVOCADO AND LEMON BASIL GRANITA

SERVES 8

LEMON BASIL GRANITA

- 2 cups water
- 3 cardamom pods, cracked
- 2 large shallots, peeled and thinly sliced
- 1 serrano chile, thinly sliced
- 1 tablespoon kosher salt
- ¼ cup sugar
- ½ pound lemon basil
- Zest of 3 lemons
- ½ cup cucumber juice (from peeled cucumber), made with a juicer
- ¼ cup champagne vinegar

COBIA

- 4 cups Pickling Marinade, divided (page 214)
- 1½ pounds cobia loin, blood line and bones removed
- 1 tablespoon kosher salt

SALAD

- 1 avocado, thinly sliced
- 3 blood oranges, peeled and sliced into 24 supremes
- 2 cups jicama, julienned
- Chile oil to taste
- Kosher salt and freshly ground black pepper
- Fresh lemon basil leaves for garnish

AVOCADO COULIS

- 1 ripe avocado, pit and skin removed
- ¼ cup water
- Juice of 2 limes
- 1 tablespoon kosher salt

PREPARE GRANITA

Place water, cardamom, shallots, chile, salt and sugar in a pot and bring to a simmer over medium-high heat. Cook for 1 minute and remove from heat.

Add basil, lemon zest, cucumber juice and vinegar; stir. Cover and let steep for 20 minutes.

Strain and place in refrigerator to chill.

Pour into a shallow glass pan and freeze for 4 hours, stirring occasionally, until liquid becomes slushy.

Every 30 minutes, use a fork to scrape the top of the granita, producing fine crystals of shaved ice, until granita is completely made up of ice crystals.

PREPARE COBIA

Set aside ½ cup marinade for the salad and bring remaining 3½ cups to a quick simmer over medium-high heat.

Season cobia with salt and slip into marinade for 30 seconds, then remove pan from heat. Transfer fish to baking dish, pour marinade over the top and chill in refrigerator so that fish is rare to medium-rare in center.

PREPARE SALAD

Remove cobia from marinade and pat dry with paper towels. Slice into thin pieces. In a bowl, mix the first 4 salad ingredients and add the sliced cobia, using some of the reserved pickling marinade to dress the salad. Season to taste.

PREPARE AVOCADO COULIS

Place all ingredients in a blender or food processer and puree until smooth. Keep chilled until ready to serve.

ASSEMBLE

In 8 very cold bowls, place a schmear of avocado coulis across the bottom. Top with salad and scoop about 1 cup granita onto each, garnishing with basil leaves. Serve immediately.

This dish has been on the menu rotation at Luma for almost five years now, and every time we take it off we hear about it. As a teenager, I was a busboy donning a tuxedo at a fancy place in Clearwater, Florida, named the Black Swan, and the waiters prepared steak tartare tableside (along with Caesar salad, crepes suzette and flaming coffees). I eagerly watched and learned how to make it all, and it has sentimental value for me, as a cook. The real surprise is the egg—a traditional part of a steak tartare preparation—which here looks almost like a Scotch egg but has a soft, runny yolk inside.

WAGYU BEEF TARTARE

WITH MALT VINEGAR, TRUFFLE CHIPS AND BLACK TRUFFLE SALAD

SERVES 4

PREPARE CHIPS

Slice potatoes paper thin on a mandoline, making sure slices are uniform. If using Yukon gold potatoes, rinse in 3 to 5 changes of cool water in a large bowl, until water is somewhat clear. Pat potatoes very dry.

Pour oil into a large pot to a depth of 3 inches. Heat to 350°F.

Working in batches of about 20 slices and returning oil to 350°F after each batch, fry potatoes, stirring gently, until golden brown, about 3 minutes.

Using a slotted spoon, transfer chips to paper towels to drain. Season each batch generously with salt and about ¼ teaspoon vinegar powder.

(Note: Chips will keep for 2 days in an airtight container at room temperature.)

PREPARE MALT VINEGAR EMULSION

Slice shallots very thinly on a mandoline; combine with malt vinegar in a medium bowl. Set aside 30 minutes. Strain and reserve vinegar.

Place egg yolks, mustard, Worcestershire sauce, ketchup, anchovy paste, Tabasco and salt in a blender. Puree on high until combined; slowly drizzle oil into blender in a thin stream. Blend until smooth.

Add reserved vinegar until consistency is similar to salad dressing. Season to taste with salt and pepper.

PREPARE SOFT-FRIED EGGS

Take eggs out of refrigerator 1½ hours before cooking.

Fill a medium saucepan with water and bring to a simmer. Add vinegar. Gently place 4 eggs into pan. Simmer 6 minutes.

Transfer eggs to a bowl of cool water until just cool enough to handle. (Do not allow to cool too much, or membrane will stick to the shell.) Gently tap each egg against a hard surface, and peel gently without breaking open. Rinse under cool water and set aside.

Pour oil into a medium pot to a depth of 3 inches. Heat to 350°F.

Place flour in a shallow dish. Break remaining 2 eggs into another shallow dish and add a small splash of milk; whisk until mostly uniform in color. Combine panko and Parmesan in a third shallow dish.

MALT VINEGAR AND TRUFFLE CHIPS

(Note: We buy Hollywood potatoes to fry exclusively because of their perfect starch-to-sugar ratio. You can easily substitute Yukon golds but will need to soak them first in a lot of water to remove all the excess starch. With the Hollywoods we go straight from slicing into the fryer.)

1¾ pounds potatoes

Vegetable oil

1 tablespoon malt vinegar powder, or to taste

Truffle salt

MALT VINEGAR EMULSION

5 large shallots

1 cup malt vinegar

4 egg yolks

3 tablespoons Dijon mustard

2½ tablespoons Worcestershire sauce

2½ tablespoons Heinz ketchup

2 tablespoons anchovy paste

2 tablespoons Tabasco sauce

1 tablespoon kosher salt, plus more to taste

3 cups grapeseed oil

Freshly ground black pepper

SOFT-FRIED EGGS

6 farm eggs, divided

1 cup white wine vinegar

Vegetable oil

1 cup all-purpose flour

1 cup panko (Japanese bread crumbs)

⅓ cup finely grated Parmesan

»

Gently roll eggs in flour, dip in egg wash, then coat with panko mixture.

Gently place eggs into hot oil, 2 at a time. Fry 1 minute. Transfer to a plate lined with paper towels until ready to serve.

PREPARE TARTARE

Refrigerate all meat-grinding equipment 1 hour before using. Grind meat with meat grinder using the medium die. Place ground meat in a large bowl; add pickles, shallots, capers, emulsion, oil, salt, chives, parsley and chili oil. Mix well. Season with additional salt and chili oil as desired.

PREPARE AIOLI

Combine lemon juice, egg yolk, garlic and truffle shavings in a blender or food processor. Blend until well combined. With blender running, add oil in a slow, thin stream. Process until thick, adding more oil as needed. Season to taste with truffle salt.

PREPARE SALAD

Drizzle frisée with just enough oil to lightly coat. Add truffle shavings, salt and chives; toss to combine.

ASSEMBLE

Place 1 teaspoon black truffle aioli on the edge of each serving plate. Using the back of a spoon, "swish" the aioli across the plate. Place 1 fried egg on each plate, followed by a small handful of black truffle salad. Evenly divide tartare among plates using a ring mold or round cookie cutter to keep a cylindrical shape. Serve with malt vinegar and truffle potato chips.

WAGYU BEEF TARTARE

12 ounces wagyu beef (such as skirt or flank), cubed

3 tablespoons kosher dill pickles, finely chopped

2 tablespoons shallots, finely diced

2 tablespoons capers, chopped

1¾ tablespoons Malt Vinegar Emulsion

1 tablespoon extra-virgin olive oil

1 teaspoon kosher salt, plus more to taste

1 teaspoon fresh chives, minced

½ teaspoon parsley, finely chopped

Chili oil

BLACK TRUFFLE AIOLI

2 teaspoons fresh lemon juice

1 egg yolk

1 medium garlic clove, finely minced

¾ tablespoon black truffle shavings

¼ cup plus 3 tablespoons extra-virgin olive oil, plus more as needed

Truffle salt

BLACK TRUFFLE SALAD

½ cup frisée, large ribs removed

Extra-virgin olive oil

12 to 16 thin shavings fresh black truffle

Pinch of truffle salt or kosher salt

1 tablespoon fresh chives, minced

SOUPS

THIRD COURSE

A great soup is more than just throwing a bunch of ingredients into a blender and hoping for the best. Soups can show the real skill of a chef, from the thoughtful combinations to the execution and presentation.

The success of a great soup starts with the broth and the base. But sometimes we'll just use plain old water because we don't want to overshadow the real star of the show—the veggies. Most of our soups are very quick dishes. They are not meant to be put into a cauldron and cooked to death. Rather, they should be cooked just long enough to capture the vibrancy of the vegetables so the ingredients can shine on their own.

I'm always asking local farmers to plant cranberry beans and other varieties of shelling beans because they are among my favorite things, and I try to make sure I have plenty of them to cook with. Since they come into season at about the same time as Florida sweet corn, it seems only natural to bring them together in this tasty soup.

CRANBERRY BEAN, CORN AND ORZO SOUP

SERVES 16

CRANBERRY BEANS

4 cups shelled fresh cranberry beans (about 3 pounds whole beans)

8 cups cold water

1 garlic clove, Microplaned

3 sprigs thyme

1 bay leaf

4 tablespoons kosher salt

½ cup extra-virgin olive oil

SOUP

1 cup yellow onion, diced ¼ inch

½ cup diced celery

½ cup diced carrot

4 garlic cloves, thinly sliced

¼ cup extra-virgin olive oil, plus 2 to 4 tablespoons for garnishing

4 cups Parmesan Stock (page 212)

4 cups fresh corn, sliced off the cob

2 cups orzo, cooked and chilled

Kosher salt and freshly ground black pepper

¼ cup basil, chopped

Freshly shaved Parmesan cheese

PREPARE BEANS

Place beans, water, garlic, thyme, bay leaf and salt in a saucepot and bring to a simmer over medium-high heat; cook until beans are tender, 15 to 20 minutes.

Drain, discarding bay leaf and thyme.

Toss beans with olive oil and reserve until ready to assemble soup.

PREPARE SOUP

In a large stockpot over low heat, sweat onions, celery, carrots and garlic in ¼ cup olive oil for 3 to 5 minutes. Add Parmesan stock and bring to a simmer over medium-high heat; simmer for 2 to 3 minutes.

ASSEMBLE

Add beans, corn and orzo to soup. Bring to a simmer. Season to taste and add basil.

Divide among hot bowls and garnish with a drizzle of extra-virgin olive oil and Parmesan.

Waterkist Farm in Sanford was one of the first farms I worked with in Central Florida. This soup is a tribute not only to the farm's wonderful array of heirloom tomatoes, but also to the fact that they would deliver them straight to the door of our restaurants every Saturday after they closed up shop at the Winter Park Farmers' Market. The secret here is to cook the tomatoes as little as possible, just enough so they release their flavor. If you don't want to go to all the trouble of making basil oil—it's fine to substitute a garnish of chopped basil and extra-virgin olive oil—this is a 20-minute recipe, tops, that you can make a day ahead of time and enjoy hot or cold.

FARMERS' MARKET TOMATO SOUP

SERVES 8

INGREDIENTS

4 pounds heirloom tomatoes, cored

4 to 5 slices firm white bread, crusts removed

2 tablespoons kosher salt, divided

¼ cup extra-virgin olive oil

5 cups thinly sliced onions (about 3 medium)

4 cups thinly sliced fennel (about 1 medium bulb)

½ cup thinly sliced garlic (about 14 cloves)

½ teaspoon chile de arbol flakes

1 cup heavy cream

Basil Oil, for garnish (page 215)

Freshly ground black pepper

METHOD

Slice tomatoes ¼ inch thick and place in a large bowl. Tear bread into pieces and place on top of tomatoes. Sprinkle with 1 tablespoon salt and set aside.

Heat olive oil in a large sauté pan over medium-low heat. Add onions, fennel, garlic and chile flakes, and slowly cook until softened but not colored. Season with remaining 1 tablespoon salt. Add tomatoes and bread to softened vegetables and mix well. Bring to a simmer and cook until tomatoes yield all their liquid, but no longer than 10 minutes.

Working in small batches, transfer one-fourth of tomato mixture to a blender. With mixer running, pour in ¼ cup heavy cream and process until smooth. Transfer to a large bowl and repeat process with remaining tomatoes and cream. Adjust seasoning to taste.

Ladle into bowls and garnish with a swirl of basil oil and freshly ground black pepper.

Florida produces an abundance of snap peas, and since they cook in a flash this soup can be ready in minutes. But if you want the soup to be a bright, vibrant green instead of a drab, Army-camo green you need to pay careful attention to chilling the soup as quickly as possible once the peas have cooked. It can then be reheated or is equally delicious cold. And to bolster that old kitchen adage "A soup is a sauce and a sauce can be a soup," it makes a great sauce for chicken or crab salad.

SUGAR SNAP PEA AND SPRING ONION SOUP

SERVES 16

INGREDIENTS

4 ounces (1 stick) unsalted butter (if serving soup cold, use ¼ cup extra-virgin olive oil instead)

2 pounds spring onions, thinly sliced

2 garlic cloves, thinly sliced

2 medium potatoes, peeled, very thinly sliced

12 cups water

2 pounds sugar snap peas, cut in ¼-inch slices

12 to 16 mint leaves, chopped

2 cups heavy cream

Kosher salt

METHOD

Over medium heat, melt butter and add onions and garlic. Cook until onions soften, about 10 minutes, making sure butter doesn't brown.

While onions and garlic are cooking, fill a large metal bowl with ice and nestle a smaller metal bowl in the ice.

When onions and garlic are softened, add potatoes and water. Bring to a simmer and cook for 15 minutes. Bring to a boil and add peas, cooking 1 minute until peas are soft. Add cream and mint leaves.

Working in batches, transfer soup to a blender, puree and pass through a sieve into the smaller metal bowl. When all the soup is in the bowl, whisk until cold, about 10 minutes. Season to taste and keep very cold until ready to serve or be reheated.

Rutabaga deserves a lot more respect than it gets. Here, its peppery bite plays nicely against the sweet potato. And the fried sage on top gives this soup a hearty taste of fall.

SWEET POTATO AND RUTABAGA SOUP

WITH CARDAMOM CRÈME FRAÎCHE AND FRIED SAGE

SERVES 16

CARDAMOM CRÈME FRAÎCHE

2 cups crème fraîche

1 teaspoon ground cardamom

Zest of 2 oranges

Generous pinch of coarse salt

SWEET POTATO AND RUTABAGA SOUP

1 bunch fresh sage leaves

½ cup (2 sticks) butter

5 garlic cloves

3 large yellow onions, peeled and thinly sliced

Pinch of sugar

3 medium sweet potatoes, peeled and thinly sliced

1 small rutabaga, peeled and thinly sliced

2 medium apples or pears, peeled and thinly sliced

Coarse salt

6 cups water

2 cups heavy cream

Apple cider vinegar

PREPARE CARDAMOM CRÈME FRAÎCHE

Place crème fraîche in a mixing bowl. Add cardamom, orange zest and salt. Whisk until firm peaks form. Refrigerate until ready to serve.

RUTABAGA DESERVES A LOT MORE RESPECT THAN IT GETS.

PREPARE SOUP

Tie sage into a small bundle with either a long sage stem or butcher's twine.

In a large pot over medium-high heat, brown butter and add sage, mopping it through the butter to coat. When sage is crisp, remove, sprinkle with salt, drain on paper towels and reserve for garnish.

Add garlic and onions to butter, stirring until softened over medium heat. Reduce heat and add sugar. Stir in sweet potatoes, rutabaga and apples or pears. Season with salt, stir and continue cooking for 10 minutes or until vegetables are tender but not soft. Add water and cream. Bring to a simmer and cook about 20 minutes.

Working in batches, ladle hot soup into a blender and puree until smooth. Strain soup through a fine-mesh sieve into a large bowl. Season to taste, adding a drop or two of apple cider, if desired.

Since my mom is a good southern lady, every New Year's Day we would have a "good-luck soup" of black-eyed peas with ham. This is my twist on it, adding a poached egg on top, which is good luck too.

PINK-EYED PEA SOUP
WITH LACINATO KALE AND POACHED EGG

SERVES 8

SOUP

½ cup extra-virgin olive oil

1 medium bunch lacinato kale, stemmed and torn in small pieces

6 garlic cloves, thinly sliced

2 cups onions, brunoise (finely diced)

1 cup celery, brunoise (finely diced)

1 cup carrots, brunoise (finely diced)

1 tablespoon ancho chili powder

4 cups fresh pink-eyed peas (or other field peas), blanched

8 cups Parmesan Stock (page 212)

Kosher salt

FOR ASSEMBLY

8 farm eggs, poached

Extra-virgin olive oil

Shaved Parmesan cheese

PREPARE SOUP

Place oil in a medium stockpot over low heat. Add kale and garlic and slowly sweat for about 45 minutes. If necessary, add a splash of water to prevent sticking. When kale is tender, add onions, celery, carrots and chili powder. Increase heat slightly and slowly cook for 5 to 10 minutes. Add peas and stock, and bring to a simmer. Season to taste with salt.

ASSEMBLE

Divide among 8 bowls, topping each serving with a warm egg. Drizzle with olive oil and sprinkle with Parmesan shavings.

CHEF'S TIP You can substitute dried or frozen peas, if fresh aren't available.

SALADS + EGGS

FOURTH COURSE

It's fair to say that I grew up on salads, and they are near and dear to me because you can take them in so many different directions beyond mere lettuce. As for eggs, they are part of many of our salads and, more than any other ingredient, they are the workhorses of our kitchen. We love to play around with eggs in every form and from all kinds of critters. Not just chickens, but ducks and sea urchins, lobster and shrimp. All good things begin with eggs.

CARLO'S
1995
OCOEE, FL

Our dear friend Denise Muir, of Rabbit Run Farm, grows amazing radishes in great abundance from fall through spring, and we created an entire salad around them. The sweetness of the pears, grapes and white balsamic vinaigrette tames the radishes and doesn't let the spiciness get out of hand. Freezing the Gorgonzola makes it easier to Microplane. We use just enough to coat every bite without overpowering.

PEAR AND RADISH SALAD
WITH GORGONZOLA

SERVES 8

PREPARE VINAIGRETTE

Marinate shallots in vinegar for 20 minutes. Slowly whisk in olive oil and season to taste.

ASSEMBLE

Mix pears, radish slices and radish quarters with arugula and grapes. Season and toss with white balsamic vinaigrette. Pull cheese from freezer and shave with a Microplane over the salad.

WHITE BALSAMIC VINAIGRETTE

2 tablespoons shallots, minced

⅓ cup white balsamic vinegar

1 cup extra-virgin olive oil

Kosher salt and freshly ground black pepper

SALAD

8 pears, quartered (we use Bosc, Seckel or Asian)

8 radishes of mixed colors, shaved on a mandoline and placed in ice water to crisp

16 radishes of mixed colors, quartered

4 ounces arugula leaves

8 ounces red or green grapes, quartered

8-ounce wedge Gorgonzola, placed in freezer for 45 minutes

RABBIT RUN FARM

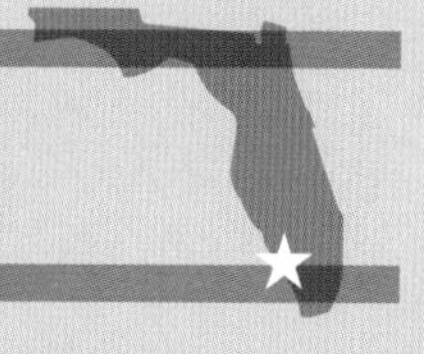

NOT LONG AFTER WE LAUNCHED Luma on Park, our friends from Gary's Seafood shared a box of produce from a new farm that had started up outside Fort Myers. Inside that box we discovered some of the best-looking veggies we had ever seen—cherry tomatoes, all kinds of lettuce, Swiss chard, kale—along with some of the sweetest strawberries imaginable.

Bright and early the next morning, I hopped in the car with Brian Cernell, our pastry chef, and we made the long haul south to meet Denise Muir of Rabbit Run Farm. She's one of those passionate, perfection-driven farmers making Florida such a great place to be a chef. Denise left her career as a financial adviser after she got frustrated trying to find decent tomatoes at the grocery store and decided to try out growing them herself. She started a hydroponic operation on two and a half acres and quickly branched out far beyond tomatoes. Rabbit Run produces vegetable varieties the skeptics told Denise she'd never be able to grow, especially in the heat of a Florida summer. She grows some varieties just for us—cranberry beans, pink-eyed peas—and if we get wild ideas about hard-to-find vegetables we'd like to play around with, she'll try to grow them for us.

We still enjoy field trips to Rabbit Run, although we have to keep an eye on Brian to make sure he doesn't go overboard "sampling" those sweet strawberries. And there's still that same sense of awe each week when we open our boxes from Rabbit Run and discover what's inside.

When I worked for Alice Waters at Chez Panisse, one of the restaurant's most iconic dishes was (and remains) a salad of baked goat cheese, shallots and field lettuces. Here is our Sunshine State version, featuring the amazing spring onions that are grown alongside strawberries. These onions are almost as sweet as the strawberries, and it's one reason why we decided to combine the two in the same dish.

STRAWBERRIES, SPRING ONIONS, TENDER LETTUCES AND FLORIDA GOAT CHEESE

SERVES 8

RED WINE VINAIGRETTE

2 tablespoons shallots, minced

⅓ cup red wine vinegar

1 cup extra-virgin olive oil

Kosher salt and freshly ground black pepper

SALAD

1 pound tender lettuces

12 ounces spring onions (about 2 or 3 medium), shaved thin on a Japanese mandoline

2 tablespoons fines herbes (parsley, thyme, chives, chervil)

2 pounds strawberries, quartered

8 ounces hazelnuts, toasted

8 ounces goat cheese

Kosher salt and freshly ground black pepper

PREPARE VINAIGRETTE

Marinate shallots in vinegar for 20 minutes. Slowly whisk in olive oil and season to taste.

ASSEMBLE

Mix lettuces, onions, fines herbes and strawberries in a bowl. Season to taste and toss with vinaigrette. Top with hazelnuts and goat cheese crumbles, then season to taste.

This is our version of a warm spinach salad. We get lacinato (aka black or Tuscan) kale in Florida almost year-round. For this recipe, I like to leave the kale a little larger instead of cutting it thin, as is often the case. This lets the true flavor and texture of the kale stand out once warmed slightly by the vinaigrette.

WARM LACINATO KALE

WITH TINY TOMATOES, PANCETTA, MANCHEGO AND CRISPY SHALLOTS

SERVES 8

PANCETTA

2 pounds pancetta, cut into ¼-inch lardons

PANCETTA VINAIGRETTE

½ cup Xérès sherry vinegar

¾ cup extra-virgin olive oil

Kosher salt and freshly ground black pepper

CRISPY FRIED SHALLOTS

2 cups canola or grapeseed oil

4 large shallots

½ cup all-purpose flour

Kosher salt and freshly ground black pepper

FOR ASSEMBLY

1 large bunch lacinato kale, stemmed, stemmed, cut into large ribbons

8 cups heirloom cherry tomatoes, halved

16 ounces Manchego cheese, shaved

PREPARE PANCETTA

Working in batches, place lardons in a large frying pan and slowly render until crispy. Drain, reserving ½ cup rendered pancetta fat and ½ cup cooked pancetta lardons for vinaigrette.

PREPARE VINAIGRETTE

Place vinegar in a small bowl and whisk in reserved ½ cup pancetta fat and the olive oil. Stir in reserved ½ cup pancetta and season to taste. Keep warm.

PREPARE SHALLOTS

Place oil in a medium-size heavy skillet and heat to 350°F. Using a Japanese mandoline, slice shallots very thin. Separate into rings and toss with flour. Shake off all excess flour and fry briefly, in batches, until brown and crispy. Drain on paper towels and season to taste.

ASSEMBLE

Place kale in a large bowl. Add tomatoes and remaining pancetta lardons. Toss with warm vinaigrette and season with salt. Divide among 8 warm bowls and top with Manchego and shallots.

When some Burrata was accidentally smashed and lost its shape, this recipe came about. Rather than let this luscious cheese go to waste, we decided to put it in a blender and use it as the base for a vinaigrette. What you have to be careful of is not to overblend or it becomes "butter," which is roughly what *burrata* means in Italian. We have an incredible melon season here in Florida, so it was a no-brainer to marry the two.

MELONS
WITH CUCUMBER, PINK PEPPERCORN AND BURRATA VINAIGRETTE

SERVES 8

VANILLA SIMPLE SYRUP

1 cup sugar

1 cup water

½ vanilla bean

MELONS

1 honeydew, quartered, seeded and peeled

1 cantaloupe, quartered, seeded and peeled

1 cup seedless red watermelon, diced ¼ inch

BURRATA VINAIGRETTE

3 ounces Burrata

2 egg yolks

1 cup white balsamic vinegar

½ cup grapeseed oil

½ cup extra-virgin olive oil

VANILLA SALT

½ cup Maldon sea salt

½ vanilla bean

FOR ASSEMBLY

2 cucumbers, peeled, seeded and thinly sliced

½ medium red onion, julienned (about 1 cup)

2 cups arugula leaves

1 cup frisée, white part only, torn into small pieces

16 ounces Burrata

2 tablespoons pink peppercorns, slightly cracked

PREPARE SYRUP

Combine sugar and water in a small pot over medium-low heat. Split vanilla bean lengthwise, scrape seeds and add to pot along with the scraped pod. Slowly bring to a simmer, stirring occasionally to dissolve sugar. Strain and chill. Keeps indefinitely.

PREPARE MELONS

Brush honeydew and cantaloupe quarters with ½ cup chilled simple syrup and wrap each quarter individually in plastic wrap.

Place watermelon in a quart vacuum bag and remove all air to compress.

Refrigerate melons overnight, up to 24 hours.

PREPARE VINAIGRETTE

Place Burrata and egg yolks in a blender and lightly combine. Add vinegar and turn blender on low speed. With machine running, slowly pour in oils. Chill.

PREPARE VANILLA SALT

Place salt in a small mixing bowl. Split vanilla bean lengthwise, scrape seeds and add to salt along with scraped pod. Mix well to evenly distribute seeds throughout salt. Spread on a small parchment-lined pan and allow to dry overnight. Transfer to an airtight container. Keeps indefinitely.

ASSEMBLE

Thinly slice honeydew and cantaloupe quarters. Divide among 8 plates, alternating and overlapping slices.

Combine cucumbers, drained watermelon, red onion, arugula and frisée in a large bowl. Toss with just enough vinaigrette to coat ingredients. Divide mixture and place on center of plated melons. Top with equal portions of Burrata.

Drizzle vinaigrette over melons and garnish with pink peppercorns and 1½ teaspoons of vanilla salt.

Tim Lovero, a Prato sous chef, inspired this recipe. We were discussing the need for a vegetable salad that could endure the heat of the grill and still remain delicious through and through. Tim went to work and upped the challenge: he made sure all ingredients went onto the grill, even the cheese, something that was new to me, reemphasizing the great benefits of team collaboration. We now use the grilled ricotta trick year-round, whenever we want to add another layer of flavor to whatever vegetables happen to be in season.

GRILLED RICOTTA SALATA
WITH SUMMER VEGETABLES, WATERCRESS AND CHARRED LEMON VINAIGRETTE

SERVES 8

SUMMER VEGETABLES

3 zucchini

3 yellow squashes

½ cup extra-virgin olive oil

Kosher salt and freshly ground black pepper

5 spring onions

1 pound green beans or wax beans

5 ears of corn

CHARRED LEMON VINAIGRETTE

6 Meyer lemons, sliced ¼ inch thick and seeded

3 tablespoons sugar

Kosher salt

1 cup extra-virgin olive oil

3 tablespoons lemon juice

4 garlic cloves, sliced paper thin

2 tablespoons champagne vinegar

PREPARE VEGETABLES

Cut zucchini and yellow squashes lengthwise into ¼-inch-thick slices. Toss with just enough oil to lightly coat, then season to taste. Grill both sides until just tender. Refrigerate until chilled.

Lightly coat onions, beans and corn with oil, and season to taste. Grill on all sides until just tender. Refrigerate until chilled.

PREPARE VINAIGRETTE

Season lemon slices with sugar and a generous sprinkling of salt, and grill until well charred on both sides. Place in a single layer on a sheet pan and refrigerate. When chilled, finely dice and place in a small bowl. Add oil, lemon juice, garlic and vinegar, and stir to mix. Season to taste.

GRILL RICOTTA

Brush ricotta slices with lemon vinaigrette and grill on both sides until marked by grill and lightly browned.

NOTE Use cheese within 1 day or cover completely with olive oil or vinaigrette and store in refrigerator.

ASSEMBLE

Julienne zucchini and squash; cut onions and beans into bite-size pieces; and cut corn kernels from cobs. Place vegetables in a large bowl and toss with 3 tablespoons vinaigrette. Add watercress to mixture and divide among individual serving plates.

Break grilled ricotta into large pieces and place on top of vegetables. Drizzle with additional vinaigrette, if desired, and season with pepper.

RICOTTA SALATA

16 ounces ricotta salata, sliced ¼ inch thick

FOR ASSEMBLY

8 ounces watercress, large stems removed

Peaches and pecans—it's Georgia on my mind. We love the marinated creamy goat feta from Australia's Meredith Dairy, but any other delicious goat feta will work. If you can't find pecan oil, just substitute (but with a gentle hand) another nut oil, or use extra-virgin olive oil.

PEACH AND RED ENDIVE SALAD WITH MARINATED FETA AND PECAN VINAIGRETTE

SERVES 8

PREPARE PECANS

Preheat oven to 300°F. Place pecans on a sheet pan and toast until slightly fragrant, 15 to 20 minutes.

PREPARE VINAIGRETTE

Pour vinegar over shallots and let sit for 20 minutes. Slowly whisk in oils and season to taste.

ASSEMBLE

Place peaches, endives and arugula in a large bowl. Season to taste. Toss with vinaigrette and divide among 8 bowls. Top each with feta and pecans.

PEACH AND RED ENDIVE SALAD

2 cups pecan halves

8 peaches, cut in small wedges

8 red Belgian endives, cored, leaves separated (radicchio may be substituted)

4 white endives, cored, leaves separated

8 cups baby arugula or lollo rosso

Kosher salt and freshly ground black pepper

16 ounces marinated feta, drained and crumbled, oil reserved

PECAN VINAIGRETTE

⅓ cup Xérès sherry vinegar

2 tablespoons minced shallots

¼ cup pecan oil

1 cup extra-virgin olive oil mixed with reserved feta oil

Kosher salt and freshly ground black pepper

This is our play on the classic French salad *frisée aux lardons*. This version got its start when we had some extra pork confit around the kitchen that we turned into rillettes and used in place of the traditional bacon—a big step up on the flavor profile. No, you don't have to use duck eggs, but it's a stylish touch if you can source them. When I'm needing comfort food for Sunday dinner, this is it.

FRISÉE SALAD
WITH PORK RILLETTE CROUTONS, FRIED DUCK EGG AND MIMOLETTE CHEESE

SERVES 8

PORK RILLETTE CROUTONS

½ teaspoon sugar

2 tablespoons kosher salt

¼ teaspoon freshly ground black pepper

4 pounds pork butt, cut into 1-inch cubes

9 garlic cloves, whole, peeled

12 to 14 sage leaves

2 bay leaves

6 cups duck fat

Breading (page 216)

Grapeseed oil

FRISÉE SALAD

¼ cup whole-grain mustard

¼ cup Banyuls vinegar (or substitute red wine or Xérès sherry vinegar)

1 cup extra-virgin olive oil

1 large bunch frisée, separated into leaves, white base removed

1 head radicchio, separated into leaves, white base removed

4 tablespoons chives, chopped

FOR ASSEMBLY

8 duck eggs, cooked sunny-side up

1 pound Mimolette cheese, shaved (can substitute Parmesan)

Kosher salt and freshly ground black pepper

PREPARE CROUTONS

Mix sugar, salt and pepper and rub into pork cubes. Add garlic, sage and bay leaves; cover and refrigerate for 8 to 24 hours.

Discard any liquid and let pork come to room temperature in a baking dish. In a large pot, warm duck fat to 110°F and pour over pork. Cover with foil and place in a 200°F oven for 3 to 4 hours, until fork-tender. Remove from oven and allow to cool for at least another 4 hours.

Remove pork cubes from fat, lightly shred and place in a bowl. Fold in at least 1 cup of the duck fat, or an amount in which any less just wouldn't be enough and any more would be grossly overindulgent. (Reserve rest of duck fat for another use.)

Roll pork into a long sausage about 3 inches in diameter and wrap in plastic wrap. Drop in an ice-water bath. When completely firm and very cold all the way through, remove pork from plastic wrap, slice into ½-inch disks and coat with breading.

In a pan over medium-high heat, fry pork slices in grapeseed oil until golden brown. Drain on paper towels; season with salt and pepper.

PREPARE SALAD

Whisk together mustard, vinegar and olive oil until well blended. Toss with frisée, radicchio and chives.

ASSEMBLE

Divide pork croutons among 8 plates and top each portion with a fried duck egg. Arrange salad around croutons. Scatter cheese on top and finish with seasoning to taste.

When I was a kid, the only way my mother could get me and my brother to eat cauliflower was to mix it with mustard, cheese and breadcrumbs. Eventually, it was a dish I grew to love—real comfort food from home.

This version, with mascarpone and crème fraîche, is rich and voluptuous. The first year it was on our menu, I probably gained 20 pounds from it alone. This tart gets more "Wows" than any dish we serve because many people are surprised that cauliflower can taste this good.

ROASTED CAULIFLOWER TART

SERVES 8

MULTIGRAIN PIE CRUST

1¼ cups all-purpose flour

½ cup whole-wheat flour

½ cup rolled oats

½ tablespoon sugar

¼ teaspoon kosher salt

12 tablespoons cold unsalted butter (½-inch pieces)

2 tablespoons ice water, plus more as needed

ROASTED CAULIFLOWER FILLING

1 head cauliflower, separated into small florets

2 tablespoons truffle oil (or olive oil)

1 large yellow onion, julienned

1 tablespoon olive oil

Kosher salt and freshly ground black pepper

2 large eggs

1 cup mascarpone

½ cup crème fraîche

1 cup grated Gruyère

1 tablespoon Dijon mustard

¼ cup Microplaned Parmesan

PREPARE PIE CRUST

Preheat oven to 375°F.

Place flours, oats, sugar and salt in a food processor and pulse until the mixture becomes a fine meal. Add cold butter and pulse until a coarse meal forms.

While machine is running, slowly add ice water until dough forms into a loose ball. Add more water as needed but do not overwork the dough into a hard mass. Shape into a flat disk and wrap tightly with plastic wrap. Refrigerate for at least 1 hour.

Divide chilled dough into 2 equal parts, freezing half for later use.

Roll out dough and place in a 9½-inch tart pan with removable bottom. Trim dough edges evenly with top of tart pan. Cover with parchment paper and fill with pie weights. Bake for 20 minutes.

Remove pie weights and parchment paper and use a fork to prick the bottom of pastry. Continue to bake until a faint golden brown, 8 to 10 minutes. Remove from oven and cool to room temperature.

PREPARE TART

Preheat oven to 325°F.

Toss cauliflower with truffle oil and season with salt and freshly ground pepper. Place in a single layer on a rimmed sheet pan and roast until cauliflower is tender and lightly caramelized, 15 to 20 minutes.

While cauliflower is roasting, caramelize onion in olive oil and season to taste.

Place eggs, mascarpone and crème fraîche in a mixing bowl and whisk until combined. Fold in Gruyère, roasted cauliflower and caramelized onions. Add 1 teaspoon salt.

Brush the bottom of multigrain pie crust with Dijon mustard. Fill crust with cauliflower mixture, level top and sprinkle with Parmesan. Bake for 35 to 40 minutes, until custard is set and cheese on top is slightly browned.

Cool to room temperature, cut into 8 pieces and serve.

LAKE MEADOW NATURALS

I DISTINCTLY REMEMBER THE FIRST TIME I MET DALE VOLKERT. It was a Saturday afternoon, shortly after Luma first opened, and the Winter Park Farmers' Market had just closed for the day. Dale came to the back door of the restaurant with some eggs he hadn't sold at the farmers' market and asked if I'd like to try them.

The rest, as they say, is history. And I've been hooked on eggs from Dale's farm—Lake Meadow Naturals—ever since.

Dale has a deep background with chickens, from the time he began raising them for 4-H projects as a boy growing up in Wisconsin. In 2000, he moved to Florida, drawn by the climate and looking for land where his cage-free chickens could roam. Dale eventually settled down on property near Lake Meadow in Ocoee, just west of Orlando, and has since expanded from chickens to include all manner of critters—ducks, turkeys, goats, rabbits and pigs—along with a vegetable farm.

Dale's place is a welcome rural oasis in the Central Florida sprawl. One of my favorite family outings is to head there with Liz and the boys. There's just something about plucking an egg fresh from the nest that is good for the soul.

Too many home cooks are scared off by soufflés. But once you make your first one, you'll discover how simple they can be to prepare. The idea of these soufflés appealed to me because it's a great way to spread a relatively small amount of stone crab, which can be pricey, among several people. If you can't find stone crab, then it's fine to substitute any other crabmeat or shrimp.

These soufflés are supposed to sink when removed from the oven, so don't be alarmed. One of the beauties of this dish is that it can be made one or two days ahead. Just pop the soufflés into the oven and heat through when ready to serve.

STONE CRAB SOUFFLÉS
WITH FINES HERBES BUTTER

SERVES 8

CAULIFLOWER PUREE

½ pound cauliflower, broken into small florets

1½ cups heavy cream

1 fresh bay leaf

1 teaspoon kosher salt

FINES HERBES BUTTER

¼ cup finely chopped shallot

½ cup apple juice

¼ cup dry white wine

¼ cup white wine vinegar

2 sticks unsalted butter

¼ teaspoon kosher salt

1 teaspoon finely chopped fresh parsley

1 teaspoon finely chopped fresh chives

1 teaspoon finely chopped fresh tarragon

PREPARE PUREE

Place cauliflower in a single layer in a saucepan and add cream, bay leaf and salt. Cover with a cartouche (parchment paper lid with a small cutout in the center) and gently simmer until tender. Remove cauliflower with a slotted spoon and place in a blender. Add just enough of the cooking cream to get the cauliflower to process. Puree until very smooth. Refrigerate until well chilled.

PREPARE FINES HERBES BUTTER

Place shallot, apple juice, white wine and white wine vinegar in a medium saucepan and bring to a simmer. Reduce until almost dry. Lower heat and add butter 1 tablespoon at a time, whisking continuously and fully incorporating each tablespoon before adding the next.

Strain butter, discarding shallots, and stir in salt. Keep in a warm spot until ready to use.

Fold the herbs into the butter just before pouring into the soufflés.

STONE CRAB SOUFFLÉS

8 tablespoons butter, divided

1 tablespoon Madras curry powder

1 tablespoon kosher salt

¼ cup all-purpose flour

1 cup Shellfish Stock, chilled (page 212)

2 egg yolks

1 cup Cauliflower Puree, chilled

1 cup stone crab meat, carefully picked through to remove shells

1 teaspoon chopped fresh parsley

1 teaspoon chopped fresh chives

1 teaspoon chopped fresh tarragon

4 egg whites

8 tablespoons Fines Herbes Butter

PREPARE SOUFFLÉS

Preheat oven to 375°F.

Melt 7 tablespoons butter in a large saucepan over medium-high heat. Add curry powder and salt, and while whisking continuously, toast until the mixture is fragrant and foaming, being careful not to burn the butter. Lower heat to medium and mix in flour. Cook at a light simmer, whisking continuously, until a rich, deep caramel color develops, about 5 minutes.

Slowly whisk in cold shellfish stock and continue to cook until the mixture is slightly thickened and smooth, and ribbons have begun to form, 2 to 3 minutes. Remove saucepan from heat. Allow mixture to cool slightly, then whisk in egg yolks, one at a time.

Add cauliflower puree and whisk to incorporate. Pour into a mixing bowl and fold in crabmeat, parsley, chives and tarragon.

Whip egg whites until stiff peaks form. Fold one quarter of egg whites into crabmeat mixture to loosen and then fold in remaining egg whites.

Use remaining butter to coat bottoms and sides of eight 3-inch ramekins. "Vertically butter" the ramekins by finishing the sides with upward strokes of a pastry brush to help soufflés rise.

Divide crab mixture equally among ramekins and gently pat tops to level.

Bake for 25 to 30 minutes, until golden brown.

ASSEMBLE

Make a small hole in the top of each soufflé, pour in 1 tablespoon herb butter and serve.

PERFECT SOFT-BOILED EGGS

Like roasting a chicken, soft boiling an egg is one of those basic kitchen skills that demands a few tried-and-true steps.

1. **USE FRESH FARM EGGS** whenever possible.
2. **REMOVE FROM REFRIGERATOR** at least 90 minutes before boiling.
3. **ADD 1 CUP WHITE WINE VINEGAR PER QUART OF WATER.** Bring water to a simmer. Water needs to remain at about 185°F throughout the process.
4. **ADD AS MANY AS 6 EGGS AT A TIME**, lowering into pot with a spider ladle.
5. **SET TIMER FOR 6 MINUTES.**
6. **WHEN TIME IS UP, REMOVE EGGS** to a slightly chilled water bath, allowing to cool just until they can be easily handled. Do not allow to overcool or membrane will stick to the albumen.
7. **GENTLY TAP EACH EGG AGAINST A HARD SURFACE** and peel gently without breaking open. Rinse under cool water and keep in ice water until needed.

195
CookTek

PASTA

FIFTH COURSE

Nothing brings me more happiness in the kitchen than making pasta. It's the simple combination of flour, egg, liquid and endless flavorings that thrills me as a chef. And there's the conviviality of it too. The daily ritual of making pasta for our ever-changing menus at Luma and Prato brings the wildly different personalities of our kitchen crew together as a team.

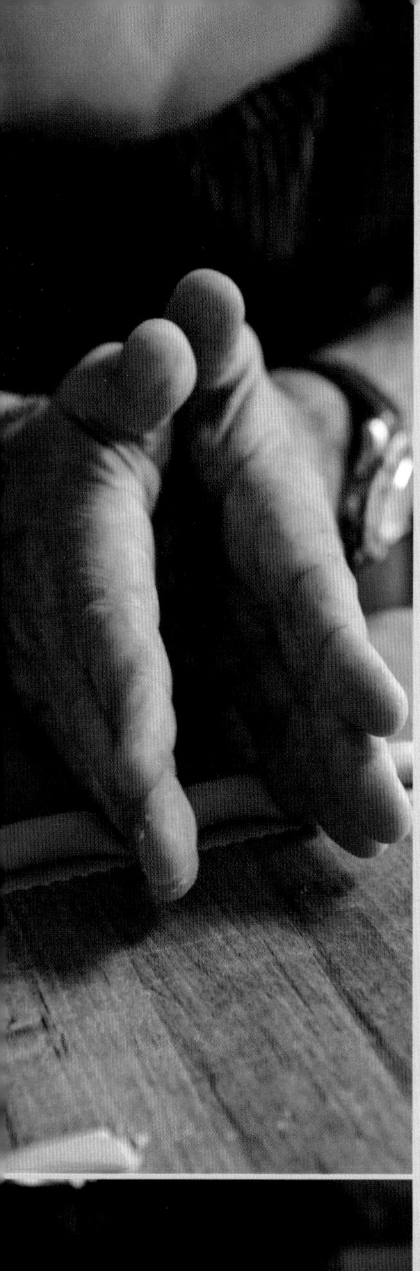

OF FLOURS AND FLAVORINGS

WE ARE CONSTANTLY SEEKING NEW APPROACHES TO PASTA (or revisiting old favorites), based on the proper ratios of flour, flavorings and hydration. The search never gets old!

When we make extruded pasta (pasta that is forced through a die to form noodles) or sheeted dough, we like to moisten it with different flavorings and colors, as a substitute for water. We've used purees made with chickpeas, lobster roe, pea shoots, sea urchin, basil, garlic, chives, squid ink, mustard powder, ramp greens—you name it. Although we religiously use the Molino Spadoni brand of flour, which hails from the Emilia-Romagna region of Italy, there are times when we will trade that in for another flour that has nuanced characteristics, such as buckwheat, whole-wheat, sunchoke, chestnut, farro, rye or truffle flours.

Making pasta at home the way we do in our kitchens is a rather simple task. The dough is usually made with a mixer and a dough hook or paddle. At home I like to use the KitchenAid extruder and roller (available at Williams-Sonoma), and I have yet to see a better model for the home cook. (I also admire the meat grinder and sausage stuffer attachments.) All recipes for this book were tested on this high-quality equipment. Beyond that:

- Use the best farm eggs and flours you can find.
- Always keep the pasta covered to prevent drying out, and if you're making filled pasta, work in small batches. We use a spray bottle filled with water to seal the edges.
- Always remove the pasta from heat before tossing in the cheese.

THE PERFECT FINISH

ONE OF THE BEST WAYS TO MAKE A GREAT PASTA DISH occurs during the final stage of cooking. When you remove the pasta from the water, it should be just 75 percent done, not quite al dente. Immediately place it in the sauce and cook the sauce onto the noodle. The noodle will release its starch and help thicken the sauce.

Make use of the pasta-boiling water if more liquid is needed (be sure not to overseason the cooking water). A great rule of thumb for pasta is that the sauce should not be running off the noodles. Instead, it should stick to them, and when you take the last bite, there should be very little residual sauce left in the bowl.

If you love a classic carbonara, then you'll appreciate our twist on it. English peas have a short growing season, so we like to extend it by using pea shoots. But truth is, peas are one of the few vegetables that work just as well frozen. While we do not substitute frozen peas in the restaurants, doing so at home is perfectly fine, sometimes even better.

PEA SHOOT TAGLIATELLE

WITH GUANCIALE, ENGLISH PEAS AND POACHED EGG

SERVES 4

PREPARE PUREE

Bring water to a boil in a large pot. Blanch pea shoots for 30 seconds until all are wilted. Drain and shock. Immediately place pea shoots in ice water to preserve color, then drain and squeeze dry, reserving some of the blanching liquid. In a blender, puree pea shoots and 3 tablespoons blanching water until smooth.

PREPARE TAGLIATELLE

Dilute salt in 1 tablespoon reserved blanching water. Add ¼ cup reserved blanching water to make green water. In a blender, mix pea shoot puree, eggs, egg yolk and green water.

Place flour in a standing mixer and slowly drizzle in the puree-egg mixture. Knead on low speed for 12 minutes.

Wrap dough in plastic wrap and flatten into a disk. Refrigerate for 30 minutes.

Remove dough from refrigerator. Using a pasta machine, roll and cut tagliatelle, following machine manufacturer's directions.

PREPARE EGGS

Add vinegar and salt to pasta cooking water. Crack eggs into the water and simmer for 3 minutes. Use a slotted spoon to transfer each egg from water to paper towels and tap excess water off. Place in ice water for 30 seconds and immediately move to slightly warm water, so they don't overcook, until pasta is ready.

FINISH TAGLIATELLE

Bring a large pot of lightly salted water to a boil.

Mix heavy cream and egg yolks together in a small bowl.

In a large sauté pan over medium-high heat, render the guanciale until crispy. Pour half of the fat out of the pan and reserve for another use.

PEA SHOOT PUREE

4 cups water

¼ pound pea shoots

PEA SHOOT TAGLIATELLE

2 teaspoons kosher salt

¼ cup plus 1 teaspoon Pea Shoot Puree

2 eggs

1 egg yolk

3 cups Molino Spadoni Premium Pasta Semolina Flour, type 00

POACHED EGGS

2 tablespoons white wine vinegar

1 tablespoon kosher salt

8 eggs

»

FOR ASSEMBLY

6 tablespoons heavy cream

6 egg yolks

1½ pounds guanciale (or pancetta/bacon)

1 pound English peas, blanched

1 tablespoon freshly ground black pepper, plus more for finish

3 ounces pea shoots

½ pound Parmesan, Microplaned

Kosher salt for finish

Add tagliatelle to the boiling water and cook for about 30 seconds. Drain in a colander, reserving the cooking water, then place pasta in pan with guanciale. Add English peas and black pepper. Add a little of the pasta water if the pasta starts to dry out. Sauté pasta over medium-high heat, 30 seconds to 1 minute, until al dente.

When pasta is al dente, add pea shoots and Parmesan and toss to combine. Reduce heat to low, slowly drizzle in egg yolk–cream mixture and immediately remove from heat.

ASSEMBLE

Divide pasta among plates. Top each plate of pasta with poached egg. Grind black pepper over top to finish; season with salt to taste.

When we're playing around with new recipes, we like to offer a little surprise while still staying true to tradition. Here the pasta filling is actually an overcooked risotto with nuts and cheese folded in. It's a dish that makes me smile.

MARCONA ALMOND CAPPELLETTI WITH CAPERS, ROASTED CAULIFLOWER FLORETS, PICKLED CURRANTS AND BROWN BUTTER

SERVES 4

PREPARE FILLING

Bring a large saucepan of water to a simmer over medium-low heat.

Heat oil in a large sauté pan; add onions and cook until golden. Add bay leaves.

Add Arborio rice, stirring to coat in oil. Add simmering water, 1 cup at a time, stirring until pan begins to look dry before adding the next cup of water. Continue adding water until rice is very soft, then continue simmering until most liquid evaporates. Remove and discard bay leaves.

Divide risotto into 3 batches. Place first batch in a food processor; add 1 egg, ⅓ of the butter, ⅓ of the mascarpone, ⅓ of the truffle oil and ⅓ of the truffle salt. Puree until smooth; transfer to a large bowl. Repeat process two more times.

Stir in Parmesan and Marcona almonds. Transfer to a piping bag and refrigerate until ready to use.

PREPARE PASTA DOUGH

Place flour in the bowl of a mixer fitted with the paddle attachment. Combine water and salt in a medium bowl, stirring until salt dissolves. Add egg and egg yolks, whisking to combine.

With mixer running, slowly add egg mixture to flour. Mix until dough begins to hold together. Turn the dough out onto a large cutting board or countertop and knead 10 minutes. Form into a ball.

Cover dough ball in plastic wrap and set aside at room temperature for at least 30 minutes.

Cut dough into 4 pieces. Using a pasta machine, roll 1 piece of dough through successively narrower settings until you begin to be able to see your fingers through the dough. The sheets should be about 5 inches wide.

Spread out the pasta sheets on a work surface lightly dusted with all-purpose flour and cover with plastic wrap. Repeat the process with remaining dough pieces.

MARCONA ALMOND FILLING

2 tablespoons extra-virgin olive oil

1½ large onions, diced

1 or 2 bay leaves

1 pound Arborio rice

3 eggs, room temperature

1 stick butter, diced, room temperature

½ cup plus 2 tablespoons mascarpone, room temperature

1 tablespoon truffle oil

1½ teaspoons truffle salt

½ cup plus 2 tablespoons grated Parmesan

1¼ pounds Marcona almonds, ground, but not to a paste

EGG PASTA DOUGH

1 pound premium 00 pasta flour

¼ cup water

1 tablespoon kosher salt

1 egg

7 egg yolks

»

PREPARE CAULIFLOWER

Preheat oven to 450°F. Toss cauliflower with a generous amount of olive oil. Spread on a large sheet pan and roast until golden brown, about 20 minutes. Season to taste and set aside.

PREPARE CURRANTS

Put pickling liquid in a small saucepan and bring to a simmer over medium-high heat. Pour liquid over currants in a small bowl. Let steep for 20 minutes.

PREPARE CAPPELLETTI

Cut pasta sheets into 1½-inch squares (keep dough, sheets and squares covered with a clean dish towel while rolling and cutting to avoid drying).

Pipe about ¼ teaspoon filling in center of each square. Rotate pasta so it's shaped like a diamond, then fold bottom corner up to meet top corner to form a triangle. Seal all edges, making sure there are no air bubbles around filling. With the triangle pointing up, slightly push the filling up with your thumb and then fold the 2 lower corners of the triangle in so that they overlap. Seal together. Keep cappelletti covered with a clean dish towel until ready to cook.

ASSEMBLE

Melt butter with salt in a large saucepan over medium-high heat. Swirl pan until butter is browned. Stir in stock and reduce heat to low.

Cook cappelletti in boiling, salted water until slightly underdone, 2 to 3 minutes. Remove and drain.

Place cappelletti in a large sauté pan. Add cauliflower, drained currants and capers. Spoon butter-stock mixture over the pasta, gently stirring to incorporate everything. Remove from heat and toss with desired amounts of parsley, lemon juice and Parmesan.

Divide among plates and garnish each plate with 3 sprigs parsley and crushed Marcona almonds.

ROASTED CAULIFLOWER

½ pound cauliflower florets

Extra-virgin olive oil

Kosher salt

PICKLED CURRANTS

1 cup Red Pickling Liquid (page 214)

½ cup dried currants

FOR ASSEMBLY

8 tablespoons unsalted butter

Pinch of kosher salt

2 cups Chicken Stock (page 212)

½ cup capers, chopped

Chopped fresh parsley

Freshly squeezed lemon juice

Finely grated Parmesan

12 sprigs fresh parsley

Crushed Marcona almonds

This came about when we had some beef trimmings left over from another dish and decided we needed to do something to jazz them up. The recipe might look daunting, but just think of it as meat and potatoes.

STUFFED POTATO GNOCCHI
WITH BEEF, FLOWERING BROCCOLI AND LOCATELLI PECORINO

SERVES 4

BEEF FILLING

1½ sticks butter, cubed

2 pounds beef top round, trimmed of fat and sinew, cut into 1½-inch cubes

Kosher salt and freshly ground black pepper

1 cup Soffrito Crudo (page 214)

20 whole garlic cloves, halved

½ cup fresh thyme leaves

2 cups dry red wine

4 cups Veal Jus (page 213)

6 ounces Parmesan, grated

3 eggs, lightly beaten

8 ounces mascarpone

1¾ cups parsley, chopped

¼ cup olive oil

GNOCCHI

4 large Russet potatoes, scrubbed

4 eggs

5 cups 00 farina flour, or as needed

Kosher salt and freshly ground black pepper

⅛ teaspoon nutmeg, grated

PREPARE BEEF FILLING

Brown butter evenly and deeply in a Dutch oven over medium-high heat.

Pat beef dry and season liberally with salt and pepper. (Season just before searing meat so as not to leach liquids from the meat.) Sear meat in browned butter over medium-high heat to brown and caramelize on each side, making sure not to cook past medium-rare in the center. (Do not overcrowd pan, or meat will steam. It is very important to not cook the meat past medium-rare, as it will change the whole dish.)

Remove meat from pan and set aside.

Add soffrito crudo to the same pan and sweat until partially cooked. After 3 or 4 minutes add garlic and then thyme. Thyme addition should create a popping sound. Add red wine and reduce by half. Add room-temperature jus and reduce by 75 percent.

Add beef with any drippings back to the pan. Stir well and cook a few minutes to reduce just a bit further. Remove mixture from pan and place in refrigerator to cool as quickly as possible.

Make sure all meat-grinding equipment is well chilled. When meat is completely chilled, remove from refrigerator, reserve juices and, using a medium (⅜-inch) die, grind meat and all vegetables into a bowl set over another bowl filled with ice. The mixture should come out like spaghetti. If it comes out in globs, stop, clean grinder parts and try again.

Place the ground meat in a chilled bowl of an electric mixer and add Parmesan, eggs, mascarpone and parsley and mix on low speed until evenly incorporated. Taste and adjust seasonings as needed.

Place mixture in piping bag and chill until ready to fill gnocchi.

PREPARE GNOCCHI

Simmer potatoes in salted water for about 30 minutes over medium-high heat. (Potatoes must be cooked all the way through to produce the right consistency of dough.)

Drain and peel potatoes while still warm. Cut into large chunks and place on a cookie sheet lined with parchment paper. Refrigerate until well chilled.

Beat eggs in a small bowl. Generously flour a work surface. Grate potatoes directly onto flour, using a food mill with a medium die. Season with salt, pepper and nutmeg. Add a little flour on top of potatoes and work it in, distributing evenly. Break up chunks to produce uniform small beads.

Make a large well in the center of potatoes and add eggs. Add more flour around the border of the potato mixture. Slowly incorporate flour from the outside in, and continue combining from outside in by using 2 bench scrapers in a chopping motion.

Continue mixing with chopping motion until potato mixture is the consistency of coffee beans. Add flour as needed to evenly distribute all ingredients. The mixture should be not too dry or too wet.

Form into a ball and knead with hands to form a solid ball that keeps its form without sagging.

Reflour the board and roll out dough, flipping partway through to allow upper surface of dough to contact floured board. The colder the dough, the easier it is to work with.

Roll to ¼-inch thickness. Sprinkle lightly with flour and cut into 3-inch rounds. Rework leftover dough, rerolling and cutting.

Pipe approximately ½ ounce (or 1-inch-round dollop) of beef filling onto each round. Fold over into half moons and seal with fingers. Crimp with a fork to seal completely, and cut off outer crimped edge with a sharp knife.

Roll each gnocchi onto its sealed edge and indent with a thumbprint to make a little boat.

Freeze for 15 minutes or refrigerate for 30 minutes.

Drop gnocchi into a large pot of boiling salted water. Cook until they float, about 3 minutes. Drain and toss with olive oil so they don't stick together. Spread out on a cookie sheet and return to refrigerator.

ASSEMBLE

Heat a thin layer of grapeseed oil in a small sauté pan over medium-high heat and toast gnocchi until all sides are nicely browned. Pour out any remaining oil and deglaze with stock.

Add jus and reduce by half. Add broccoli rabe and toss with the sauce. Taste for seasoning and adjust as needed. Add chile flakes to taste, if using.

Divide gnocchi, broccoli and sauce among plates and garnish with Pecorino Romano and minced chives.

FOR ASSEMBLY

¼ cup grapeseed oil

½ cup Chicken Stock (page 212)

½ cup Veal Jus (page 213)

1 pound broccoli rabe florets, blanched and shocked in ice water

Kosher salt

Chile de arbol flakes (optional)

1 pound Locatelli Pecorino Romano, Microplaned

½ cup minced chives

You can make the cavatelli ahead of time and freeze it until needed. Just make sure not to defrost the cavatelli before cooking. Add them frozen, directly to the pot. And as an alternative to using individual plates, you can assemble this as a casserole to serve to your guests.

BLACK TRUFFLE–RICOTTA CAVATELLI WITH TURKEY LEG CONFIT

SERVES 4

TURKEY LEG CONFIT

2 tablespoons kosher salt

1 teaspoon sugar

½ teaspoon freshly ground black pepper

1 turkey leg with thigh attached

Duck fat (approximately 4 cups)

BLACK TRUFFLE–RICOTTA CAVATELLI

2 teaspoons truffle oil

½ cup black truffle peelings

1 cup ricotta

3 egg yolks

1 teaspoon kosher salt

½ garlic clove, Microplaned

1¾ cups premium 00 pasta flour

⅔ cup semolina flour

1 tablespoon plus 1 teaspoon truffle flour (can substitute 00 flour)

¼ teaspoon ground black pepper

BLANCHED LEEKS

2 leeks, white part only

2 tablespoons kosher salt

PREPARE CONFIT

Combine seasonings and coat turkey leg with mixture. Place in a plastic container and refrigerate for 24 hours.

The next day, remove turkey leg from refrigerator and let sit at room temperature for 1 hour.

Preheat oven to 225°F.

Place turkey leg in a 2-quart casserole dish. Warm enough duck fat to cover turkey leg. Pour duck fat over turkey leg and cover dish with foil.

Bake for 3 to 4 hours, until meat falls from the bone. Allow to rest in fat for at least 6 hours. Pull meat from bones. (Can be prepared up to 2 weeks in advance.)

PREPARE CAVATELLI

Place truffle oil and truffle peelings in a food processor and chop until fine, scraping sides to make sure everything is well ground. Add ricotta, egg yolks and salt, and puree until well incorporated.

Place truffle mixture in a mixing bowl and add garlic, flours and pepper. Mix and form into a ball.

Place on a floured surface and knead for 2 minutes until smooth and elastic, adding more flour to keep from sticking if necessary. Roll dough flat, about ½ inch or smaller. Wrap in plastic wrap and refrigerate for at least 1 hour.

Dust a cookie sheet with semolina flour. Unwrap dough and place under a damp cloth on top of a floured surface. Divide dough into 12 pieces and roll each one into a long, narrow rope about the size of a wooden spoon handle. Cover ropes with damp cloth.

Using a small knife, slice off enough dough to roll into the size of a chickpea. Drag the dough across a ridged cavatelli board with your thumb. The pasta will curl up, creating the cavatello shape. Or, if you have a cavatelli machine, follow directions accordingly.

Place on a wire rack and continue with remaining of dough.

PREPARE BLANCHED LEEKS

Slice leeks in half lengthwise, then slice into ¼-inch half-moons. Rinse well in a water bath. Skim slices off the top without disturbing the dirt below.

Bring a large pot of water to a boil and add salt. Blanch leeks until tender, about 30 seconds to 1 minute, then drain.

Shock leeks in an ice water bath. Drain and dry thoroughly with paper towels.

ROBIOLA FONDUTA

3 egg yolks

1 tablespoon plus 1 teaspoon cornstarch

10½ ounces Robiola Bosina, room temperature

1 cup whole milk

Kosher salt and white pepper

Black truffle shavings (optional)

FOR ASSEMBLY

Black truffle for grating (optional)

Pangrattato (page 216)

Parmesan, Microplaned

PREPARE ROBIOLA FONDUTA

Whisk egg yolks and cornstarch together in a saucepan over low heat, stirring constantly until thick. Remove from heat and stir in Robiola.

Let rest for 5 minutes and transfer to a blender. Puree until smooth.

Pass through a strainer and season to taste. Fold in truffle shavings, if using. Keep covered in a warm spot.

ASSEMBLE

Preheat oven to 400°F.

In a large pot of boiling salted water, blanch cavatelli for 3 to 4 minutes, until they float. Drain, place in a room-temperature sauté pan and return to stove over medium-low heat.

Add 6½ ounces turkey meat and ½ cup blanched leeks to fonduta. Watching constantly, keep moving and tossing the mixture until warm. (Be careful, as continuous heat can make it curdle.) Adjust seasonings as needed. Place in individual cast-iron dishes (or casseroles). Ladle a little more fonduta over tops (it will later form into a bubbly sauce). Top with truffle, if using, pangrattato, then Parmesan. Bake for 5 to 10 minutes until bubbling and golden brown.

imperia
Restaurant

We're always looking for new ways to flavor pastas before we toss them with the sauce. Sea urchin adds the briny flavor of the sea and it gives the pasta an inviting golden hue. Finishing it with Cortez bottarga, a cured Florida mullet roe, brings home a taste of the Gulf of Mexico. We source fresh sea urchin that's already prepared and ready to eat. It's easy to obtain through local specialty stores or online.

SEA URCHIN RIGATONI
WITH GARLIC, LEMON AND PANGRATTATO

SERVES 4

SEA URCHIN RIGATONI

4½ ounces sea urchin roe (uni)

1 garlic clove, Microplaned

½ tablespoon salt

¼ cup water

1 egg

5 egg yolks

3½ cups plus 1 tablespoon Premium Pasta Blend (page 216), plus extra for dusting

FOR ASSEMBLY

¾ cup extra-virgin olive oil

10 garlic cloves, thinly sliced

1 chipotle pepper (or fresh jalapeño)

2 cups Parmesan, Microplaned

1 cup basil, chopped

½ cup lemon juice

8 to 16 sea urchins, whole, about ½ to 1 ounce each (the more the better!)

Freshly shaved Cortez bottarga

Pangrattato (page 216)

PREPARE RIGATONI

In a blender, combine uni, garlic, salt, water, egg and egg yolks. Puree until smooth.

In a standing mixer fitted with the hook attachment, add pasta flour and slowly drizzle in uni mixture until well combined.

Turn dough out onto a smooth surface, using pasta flour as needed so it doesn't stick, and knead for 8 minutes. Shape into a disk and wrap in plastic. Let rest for 30 minutes in the refrigerator.

Remove dough from refrigerator. Using the rigatoni die on a pasta machine and following manufacturer's directions, extrude dough onto a cookie sheet sprinkled with semolina flour.

ASSEMBLE

Bring a pot of lightly salted water to a boil.

In a sauté pan, warm olive oil over medium heat and cook garlic and chipotle until soft.

Drop rigatoni in water and cook for 2 to 3 minutes. Remove rigatoni from water and drain, reserving some of the pasta water.

Place rigatoni in sauté pan. Add a little of the pasta water to finish cooking. When rigatoni is al dente and the sauce/oil has been cooked into the pasta, add Parmesan and basil.

Check for seasoning, adjust as needed and finish with lemon juice.

Divide among bowls and top each with fresh sea urchins, shaved bottarga and pangrattato.

Throughout the year we can rely on getting amazing clams from Cedar Creek Shellfish, which harvests from beds in Mosquito Lagoon. What sets these clams apart is that Cedar Creek goes to great lengths to purge the clams to remove sand, which makes it much easier on our end. Still, I've included the purging technique here to guarantee that you don't have to deal with the grit.

ALEPPO PEPPER BUCATINI
WITH CEDAR CREEK CLAMS, GUANCIALE AND ZELLWOOD CORN

SERVES 4

ALEPPO PEPPER BUCATINI

- 2 teaspoons kosher salt
- ¾ cup water
- ½ cup Aleppo pepper
- 1 egg
- 2 egg yolks
- 3½ cups plus 1 tablespoon Premium Pasta Blend (page 216)

CLAM BROTH

- 8 dozen clams
- ¼ cup cornmeal
- 1 cup shallots, sliced thin
- 3 bay leaves
- 2 tablespoons butter
- 1 (750-milliliter) bottle dry white wine

FOR ASSEMBLY

- 1 pound guanciale (can substitute pancetta tessa or bacon)
- 1 cup reserved clam liquid
- 1¼ cups Zellwood corn
- 1¼ cups wax beans, cut on bias in half
- ½ pound Parmesan, Microplaned
- 1 tablespoon chives, diced

PREPARE BUCATINI

In a small saucepot over medium-high heat, bring salt, water and Aleppo pepper to a simmer. Transfer to a blender and puree for 1 minute. Pass through a sieve and chill immediately.

Place pasta flour in a medium bowl.

When pepper mixture is cold, add egg and egg yolks and stir. Slowly drizzle the liquid into the flour, mixing with a wooden spoon.

On a floured surface, knead dough for 12 minutes. Flatten into a disk and wrap in plastic wrap. Refrigerate for 1 hour.

Follow your pasta machine's directions for extruding bucatini.

PREPARE CLAM BROTH

In a large bowl of cold water, rinse clams three times. Discard water, place clams back in bowl and cover with cold water. Sprinkle cornmeal over the water to help expel any sand and refrigerate for 45 minutes. Remove clams from refrigerator, rinse in clean water again and drain.

In a large Dutch oven, sweat shallots and bay leaves in butter for 3 minutes. Add clams and white wine. Cover and steam until all clams have opened. Strain, reserving liquid and clams separately.

Pass the liquid through 4 layers of damp cheesecloth to remove any undesired solids.

Pick meat from clams. Reserve meat and discard shells, shallots and bay leaves.

ASSEMBLE

Bring a large pot of lightly salted water to a boil.

In a sauté pan, render guanciale over medium heat until crispy. Drain fat, returning guanciale to pan.

Add clam liquid to guanciale and bring to a simmer.

Drop bucatini into pot of boiling water and cook for about 1 minute. Remove bucatini and place directly in sauté pan, finishing it in the clam broth.

When bucatini is al dente, add clams, corn and wax beans.

Return to a simmer. Add more salt, if desired.

Divide among bowls. Finish with Parmesan and chives.

This dish has been on the menu at Luma since we opened, and it has developed its own cult following. It was inspired by the famous four-hour ragout from San Francisco's Delfina Restaurant, which we turned into a six- to eight-hour ragout to make it even richer. Here we make garganelli, because we like how the sauce sticks to the ribs and melds with the pasta.

BOLOGNESE
WITH PORCINI GARGANELLI

SERVES 8

PREPARE BOLOGNESE SAUCE

Place oil in a large sauté pan and heat until shimmering. Add pork and beef in batches, breaking up meat with a wooden spoon as it sears. Season with at least ½ tablespoon salt and continue breaking up meat as much as possible.

Add chicken livers and stir into meat. The mixture will start to stick to the bottom of the pan at this point, so work fast and stir constantly. Cook for 1 minute.

Add onions, celery, carrot, garlic, porcini powder and chile flakes. Lower heat and continue to cook for about 5 minutes, constantly scraping bottom of pan with wooden spoon to release any carmelization. Add more oil if needed. Add an additional ½ tablespoon of salt.

Add tomato paste, anchovy paste and tomatoes. Stir well to blend and cook about 5 minutes, stirring frequently.

Add bay leaves, parsley and thyme. Mix well and then turn up heat to aid vegetables in releasing their sugars.

Add red wine and reduce by half, constantly scraping sides of pan. Reduce heat to a slow simmer and add milk, cream and chicken stock. Slowly simmer, stirring frequently, for 6 hours.

Chill and let rest overnight to develop flavors (though sauce can be eaten immediately).

(Note: This recipe makes far more than needed for 8 appetizer portions, but it freezes well for another occasion.)

BOLOGNESE SAUCE

2 tablespoons olive oil
1½ pounds pork butt, ground
½ pound beef (skirt, flank or tri-tip), ground
Kosher salt
¼ pound chicken livers, pureed
1 cup onion, finely diced
½ cup celery, finely diced
½ cup carrot, finely diced
5 garlic cloves, thinly sliced
1½ tablespoons porcini powder
¾ teaspoon chile de arbol flakes
1 tablespoon tomato paste
2 teaspoons anchovy paste
1 cup canned San Marzano crushed tomatoes, pureed
½ cup Italian parsley, chopped
2 bay leaves
1 tablespoon fresh thyme, chopped
½ (750-ml) bottle dry red wine
1 cup whole milk
¼ cup heavy cream
2 cups Chicken Stock (page 212)

PORCINI GARGANELLI

1½ tablespoons porcini powder

1 tablespoon kosher salt

¼ cup water

1 egg

7 egg yolks

3½ cups premium 00 pasta flour

Semolina flour for rolling and cutting

FOR ASSEMBLY

2 tablespoons kosher salt

½ cup dry red wine

1 stick butter

½ pound Parmesan, Microplaned

¼ cup Italian parsley, chopped

PREPARE PORCINI GARGANELLI

Whisk together porcini powder and salt in water to dissolve. Mix in egg and egg yolks, making sure to break up eggs.

Place flour in a mixer fitted with the paddle attachment. Slowly pour egg mixture into flour, combining on low speed. Mix for 2 to 3 minutes.

Bring dough together in a tight ball and turn out onto a floured surface. Knead for 9 to 10 minutes, until dough is smooth and springs back when poked. Wrap dough ball in plastic wrap. Using a rolling pin or your hands, flatten dough roll to a ½-inch-thick square, so dough fits into pasta machine. Let rest for 30 minutes in plastic wrap.

Divide dough into 8 portions. Roll each portion out to the thinnest setting on a pasta machine. Sprinkle each sheet of pasta with pasta flour to prevent sticking and cover with a cloth while rolling the garganelli.

Cut pasta into 2-inch squares, a few at a time so they don't dry out. Place one square on a garganelli board with one of the corners toward you, and place the dowel horizontally at the top corner of the pasta square. Roll dowel down toward yourself, pressing slightly to create ridges. At the bottom, pick up bottom corner of pasta, then roll dowel back up, away from you.

Slide pasta from dowel, maintaining shape, and place on a dusted cookie sheet. Now that pasta is formed, we encourage pasta to dry out some. Repeat with remaining squares.

ASSEMBLE

In a large pot, bring 6 quarts water to a boil with salt.

In a smaller pot, bring 3 cups Bolognese sauce, red wine and butter to a light simmer over medium heat.

When water is at a rolling boil, drop garganelli into water for 30 seconds. Drain and add to the Bolognese sauce, adding a little pasta cooking water if needed.

Mix pasta and sauce and add salt to taste. Fold in Parmesan.

Divide among bowls and garnish with chopped parsley.

No, this isn't simple, but it is one of the most requested dishes at Luma from November through January (when chestnuts are in season), and we had to include it here. It's so popular, we use a similar recipe at Prato, with the chestnut filling on crostini and served with braised short ribs. Once you master the recipe, you'll have it down, and you'll want to make it again and again. If there is one dish in this book that says "luxury," this is it.

CHESTNUT AGNOLOTTI
WITH RED WINE–BRAISED OXTAIL AND POACHED MARROW

SERVES 4

POACHED MARROW

5 (8-inch) beef marrow bones, canoe-cut

1 cup salt

1 gallon water

BRAISED OXTAILS

6 pounds oxtails, approximately 2 to 3 inches thick

1 tablespoon kosher salt

2 teaspoons freshly ground black pepper

1 cup flour

¼ cup grapeseed oil (or canola oil)

3¼ cups carrots, peeled, thinly sliced

2½ cups celery, thinly sliced

8 cups onions, thinly sliced

15 garlic cloves, peeled

2½ cups cremini mushrooms, quartered

2 (750-milliliter) bottles dry red wine

3 bay leaves

3 rosemary sprigs

8 thyme sprigs

5 cups Veal Jus (page 213)

»

PREPARE BONE MARROW

With marrow bones at room temperature, take a spoon and scoop the length of the bones to remove marrow in one piece.

Drop marrow into an ice bath of half water and half ice for 24 to 48 hours, until all the blood and impurities are extracted. The ice water should be changed 2 or 3 times daily during this process.

When process is complete, remove marrow from water and dice into ½-inch cubes. Keep marrow ice-cold and then blanch for 20 to 30 seconds in boiling salted water.

Drain and immediately place marrow cubes back in an ice water bath. Store in very cold water (without ice) until ready to use.

PREPARE OXTAILS

Liberally season oxtails with salt and pepper and refrigerate overnight. The next day, dry each oxtail with a paper towel, dust with flour and tap the meat to remove any excess flour.

In a large ovenproof pot, heat oil over medium-high heat until shimmering. Cooking in batches if necessary, place oxtails in oil in 1 layer, meat side down, starting with the larger pieces, which take longer to brown. After browning begins, turn each piece with tongs to ensure even browning on all sides.

Transfer oxtails to a colander to drain excess oil. Keep warm.

Preheat oven to 325°F.

In the pot with remaining fat, add carrots, celery, onions, garlic and mushrooms. Sauté for 5 minutes, until vegetables are soft and fragrant. Add wine and simmer until reduced by 25 percent.

Add oxtails, bay leaves, rosemary, thyme and veal jus. Mix well. Cover with a piece of parchment paper and press it down over the meat.

Bring to a simmer. Cover pot tightly with foil. Place in oven and braise for 3 to 4 hours, until fork-tender.

Uncover and allow oxtails to cool to room temperature while still in the braising liquid.

Remove oxtails from braising liquid and place on a cookie sheet. Taste and season as needed. Cover oxtails with plastic wrap and refrigerate overnight. Skim fat from braising liquid and discard.

Strain braising liquid and place in a pot on the stove over medium-high heat. Reduce by about half, until it coats the back of a spoon. Refrigerate overnight.

The next day, pick meat from oxtails, leaving in chunks rather than shredding. Set aside, discarding fat and bones.

PREPARE CHESTNUT CREAM

In a large Dutch oven, brown butter over medium-high heat. When color is dark brown and butter smells nutty, immediately add onions to the pan. Season with salt and caramelize onions, about 30 to 40 minutes. Add chestnuts, garlic, sachet, bay leaf and cream.

Cook on low, occasionally scraping bottom of Dutch oven with a rubber spatula, until cream has almost evaporated. Remove rosemary sachet. Transfer to a bowl and keep warm.

PREPARE CHESTNUT FILLING

Place all ingredients in a food processor and puree for 2 minutes. Scrape down sides and puree again until completely smooth. Divide mixture into 2 piping bags fitted with large tips and place in refrigerator to cool.

PREPARE EGG PASTA DOUGH

Whisk together salt and water to dissolve. Mix with egg and egg yolks, making sure to break up eggs. Place flour in a mixer fitted with the paddle attachment.

With mixer on lowest speed, slowly pour egg mixture into flour and mix until blended, 2 to 3 minutes.

Turn out dough onto a floured wooden board and knead for 9 to 10 minutes, until dough is smooth and springs back when poked. Wrap the dough ball in plastic. Using a rolling pin or your hands, flatten dough roll to a ½-inch-thick square, so dough fits into pasta machine. Let rest for 30 minutes in plastic wrap.

PREPARE AGNOLOTTI

Divide pasta into 8 pieces. Run one piece through a pasta maker, according to manufacturer's instructions, at the second-thinnest setting.

Lay pasta sheet on floured board and cut pasta into rectangular sheets about 12 inches long. Sprinkle flour lightly on each sheet. Continue with remaining pasta, stacking the floured rectangles.

Place one sheet of pasta on board, with one long edge toward you. Pipe a straight line of chestnut filling lengthwise on the pasta sheet, about 1 inch from top edge, leaving enough pasta at the top to fold over the filling.

Brush a little water along the top edge of the pasta to create a seal when folded. Fold the pasta top over the filling. Press firmly to seal.

Using a wheeled pasta cutter, cut the filled tube of pasta away from the rest of the sheet, making sure to keep the sealed strip intact and leaving ½ inch of seal.

Pinch the tube of pasta into 1-inch sections, creating a seal between pockets of filling. Use the wheeled pasta cutter to separate the sections.

Place finished agnolotti on a cookie sheet sprinkled with flour. Repeat until all of the pasta sheets and filling have been used.

ASSEMBLE

Boil lightly salted water and cook agnolotti for 1½ minutes. Drain.

Place agnolotti in a sauté pan along with the braised oxtail, braising liquid and mirepoix. Cook agnolotti in sauce for 30 seconds, until heated through. Add cubes of marrow. Continue to cook until marrow is just warmed through but not melted.

Divide among plates. Garnish with Manchego shavings.

HOT CHESTNUT CREAM

1 stick butter

1 pound yellow onions, thinly sliced

1 teaspoon salt

2 pounds chestnuts, roasted and shelled

3 garlic cloves, thinly sliced

½ rosemary sprig, in a sachet

1 bay leaf

2 cups heavy cream

CHESTNUT FILLING

Hot Chestnut Cream

1 cup mascarpone

2 eggs

2 teaspoons truffle oil

½ teaspoon truffle salt

EGG PASTA DOUGH

1 tablespoon kosher salt

¼ cup water

1 egg

7 egg yolks

3¾ cups premium 00 pasta flour

FOR ASSEMBLY

20 chestnut agnolotti

4 cups braised oxtails

1½ cups braising liquid

½ cup Glazed Soffrito (page 214)

32 cubes poached marrow

Manchego shavings

CHARCUTERIE

SIXTH COURSE

Crafting house-made charcuterie has gained a lot of steam in American restaurants in recent years as we see the wisdom in using all parts of an animal. No, it's not a simple process, but it is certainly within reach of the home chef. As with all things, practice makes you better. And even if you make mistakes, they are still good to eat.

Fleetwood
SKYMSEN

When Chef Matt Cargo and I were traveling around Italy to get ideas for Prato, we ate at an amazing bistro in Bologna and were so blown away by the pork belly pancetta that we made reservations for a second evening in hopes of getting to know the owners. After a couple of grappas, they agreed to share their recipe. When we got home we got all poetic with our own version of the dish and switched the pork belly to veal breast, which is also known as veal belly. Here we cure, sear, wrap in a plastic roulade and slow cook the veal belly in water. At the restaurant, when we want to give it the proper pastrami treatment, we cold smoke it an hour before or after cooking.

VEAL BREAST PASTRAMI

WITH ROASTED BEETS, HORSERADISH AND CRÈME FRAÎCHE

SERVES 8
WITH PLENTY OF LEFTOVERS

NOTE *You'll need to start this recipe at least 3 days in advance in order to cure the veal breast. This will make more than you need for 8 appetizer servings, but it keeps well, is good in sandwiches or can be frozen.*

VEAL BREAST PASTRAMI

1½ cups kosher salt

1½ cups sugar

1 teaspoon Sel Rose No. 1 (we source from D'Artagnan)

2 tablespoons fresh oregano, chopped

1 tablespoon fresh rosemary, chopped

1 (4- to 5-pound) veal breast

¾ cup Activa RM

2 tablespoons grapeseed or canola oil

ROASTED BEETS

2 pounds beets, various colors

1 cup water

¼ cup red wine vinegar

¼ cup plus 2 tablespoons white wine vinegar, divided

⅛ cup extra-virgin olive oil

5 sprigs fresh thyme

3 bay leaves

Kosher salt and black pepper

3 tablespoons olive oil

»

PREPARE PASTRAMI

Mix salt, sugar, Sel Rose and herbs in a large bowl. Rub veal breast well with mixture. Wrap in plastic and refrigerate for 2 days.

On the third day, remove from wrap and pat dry with paper towels. Sprinkle meat with Activa. Form breast into a tight roll and truss with butcher's twine. Refrigerate veal breast uncovered overnight.

The next day, remove rolled breast from refrigerator and let come to room temperature. Heat oil in a large sauté pan and sear roll on all sides. Wrap securely in layers of plastic wrap, tying ends tightly.

In a large pot over low heat, with a thermometer monitoring the water temperature, poach roll in 155°F water for 2½ hours or until internal temperature reaches 145°F.

Remove from water and let rest 30 minutes. Place in an ice water bath and refrigerate until ready to serve.

PREPARE BEETS

Preheat oven to 325°F.

Cut tops off beets and reserve for another use. Rinse beets well.

Separate beets by color first and then size, if uneven. Place beets in 2 baking pans, reds in one and light colors in the other.

Add ¼ inch water to pans. Add vinegars—red wine vinegar to red beets and ¼ cup white wine vinegar to light colors—along with extra-virgin olive oil. Add thyme sprigs and bay leaves and season with salt and pepper to taste. Cover with foil and place in oven.

Bake for 30 minutes or until easily pierced by a knife. Using a towel to hold them, peel beets by rubbing with your fingers. The skin should fall away easily.

Slice beets on a mandoline to ⅛-inch thickness. Refrigerate.

Whisk together remaining 2 tablespoons white wine vinegar and the olive oil, then season to taste. Marinate beets in vinaigrette until ready to serve.

FOR ASSEMBLY

½ pound arugula

¼ cup fresh horseradish, Microplaned, or 1 tablespoon prepared

¼ cup crème fraîche

ASSEMBLE

Thinly slice pastrami and divide among plates. Arrange beets around pastrami. Garnish with arugula, Microplaned fresh horseradish and crème fraîche. (If using prepared horseradish, mix with crème fraîche before plating for an equal distribution.)

At Prato, we like to roast the foie gras lobes in the wood oven at a very high temperature. But if a wood oven is unavailable, you can use a grill—just beware of flare-ups because of the high fat content in the foie gras. We use the roulade technique to shape into a circular presentation, but a square terrine mold can always be substituted. Each lobe of foie gras is a different size so please adjust the recipe accordingly. We buy our foie gras for Prato and Luma from LaBelle Farms in Ferndale, New York.

GRILLED FOIE GRAS TERRINE
WITH GUINNESS WAFFLES AND FIG RELISH

SERVES 16

FOIE GRAS

1 pound foie gras

1¼ teaspoons salt

½ teaspoon Sel Rose No. 1

½ teaspoon sugar

¼ teaspoon freshly ground white pepper

2 tablespoons port

2 teaspoons red wine

»

PREPARE FOIE GRAS

Rinse foie gras in cold water and pat dry with paper towels. Separate lobes and remove fat membrane.

Mix together salt, Sel Rose, sugar and pepper. Season foie gras with mixture.

Mix together port and red wine. Place foie gras in a Cryovac bag and pour port mixture over lobes. Seal bag and refrigerate overnight.

The next day, transfer foie gras to counter and let rest for 1 hour.

Preheat oven to 300°F. Heat a grill to the maximum setting.

Dry foie gras with paper towels. Turn off flame to avoid flare-ups and grill foie gras. Using tongs and a spatula, turn foie gras to color with grill marks and add a smoky flavor on each side.

In a large pan over high heat, quickly sear foie gras on each side to add more color to the lobe. Bake in oven for 3 minutes or until slightly firm to the touch.

Remove and let cool for 30 minutes.

Gently open each lobe of foie gras with your fingers. Locate the larger vein that splits into 2 directions inside the lower part. Using a pair of tweezers, carefully remove the center vein from the foie gras. Reassemble lobe to its former shape and refrigerate for 1 hour.

Place foie gras on a long sheet of plastic wrap. Wrap short ends around foie gras and gather long ends in both hands. Twist plastic wrap at each end multiple times, squeezing foie gras into a tube shape. Roll tightly until foie gras resembles a cylinder. Using a sharp knife tip, prick the plastic where air bubbles have appeared. Tie off each end of plastic wrap with butcher's twine.

Place in an ice water bath for 2 hours to firm. Refrigerate overnight.

PREPARE FIG RELISH

Place duck fat, shallot and onion in a medium saucepot over medium heat. Sweat vegetables slowly to avoid coloring, 4 to 5 minutes.

Add vinegar and honey and bring to a simmer. Add figs and let simmer gently, making sure mixture does not stick to the bottom.

Cook for 20 to 30 minutes, until liquid has evaporated. Season to taste.

PREPARE GUINNESS WAFFLES

Preheat waffle iron.

Mix flour, cornstarch, baking powder, baking soda, salt and sugar in a bowl. Whisk together milk, eggs and Guinness in a second bowl. Combine wet and dry ingredients and mix well. Whisk in oil, being careful not to overmix.

Pour ½ cup batter into center of waffle iron and spread until within ½ inch of rim, adding more if needed.

Close iron and cook 2 to 3 minutes, until deep golden brown.

ASSEMBLE

Unwrap foie gras. Dip a sharp knife in boiling water to heat blade. Slice foie gras into ½-inch slices, reheating knife between slices.

Place 1 slice foie gras on each plate. Top with 1 tablespoon relish.

Cut waffles into 4 triangles and fan out, like a deck of cards, to one side of foie gras.

BLACK MISSION FIG RELISH

2 tablespoons duck fat

5½ ounces shallot, diced

5½ ounces red onion, cut into bruinoise

1½ cups Banyuls vinegar

1⅓ cups acacia honey

3⅓ pounds black mission fig, diced

Kosher salt and freshly ground black pepper

GUINNESS WAFFLES

2 cups Guinness Draught

3½ cups flour

1 cup cornstarch

2 teaspoons baking powder

1 teaspoon baking soda

2 teaspoons kosher salt

6 teaspoons sugar

2 cups milk

4 eggs

1⅓ cups vegetable oil

This recipe is straight out of Paul Bertolli's *Cooking by Hand*. It's one of the bibles of our kitchen and should be in the library of any aspiring chef. This dish is so perfect that we could never stray from the amazing original recipe that Bertolli created.

PANCETTA TESA

MAKES 6 POUNDS

INGREDIENTS

2 tablespoons whole black peppercorns

7 whole cloves

3 allspice berries

1 teaspoon freshly grated nutmeg

1 tablespoon red pepper flakes

7 juniper berries

⅓ cup kosher salt

1 teaspoon Insta Cure No. 1 (or other pink curing salt)

6 pounds pork belly, skin on, 40 percent lean

5 garlic cloves, Microplaned

¼ cup red wine

METHOD

Combine peppercorns, cloves, allspice berries, nutmeg, pepper and berries in a spice grinder and grind until coarse meal is produced. Combine ground spices and salts.

Place pork belly in a large square pan and rub spice mixture liberally and evenly into the meat, using all of the mixture.

Combine garlic and wine and lightly sprinkle over both sides of the meat so as not to wash away the spicing.

Cure for 8 to 15 days in refrigerator set below 40°F.

The tesa is ready when salts have penetrated to the center of the belly. Test for doneness by tasting a thin slice. (If you'd rather not eat it raw, crisp first in a sauté pan.) Tesa will keep for up to 30 days if well refrigerated, and may be frozen as well. To freeze, wrap well in freezer paper and store in a zip-top bag.

A lot of recreational hunters frequent our restaurants, and all of them brag about their "secret sausage." They inspired us to create our own version. Here, the underlying flavors of cocoa, ancho, coffee and peppercorn are all good flavor pals to the venison's gamey nuances.

VENISON SAUSAGE APPLE–COCOA NIB SALAD

AND BLACK PEPPERCORN–COFFEE GASTRIQUE

SERVES 8 TO 10

EQUIPMENT Meat grinder, sausage stuffer, Japanese mandoline

VENISON SAUSAGE

2½ pounds venison shoulder or leg

¾ pound pork fatback

3½ tablespoons kosher salt

¾ teaspoon sugar

1 tablespoon garlic, Microplaned

1 tablespoon pimiento picante

1½ teaspoons cocoa powder

1 teaspoon ancho chili pepper powder

2½ tablespoons red wine, ice-cold

1 tablespoon red wine vinegar, ice-cold

2 tablespoons water, ice-cold

Hog or sheep casings

TELLICHERRY PEPPERCORN–COFFEE BEAN GASTRIQUE

6 tablespoons Tellicherry peppercorns, slightly cracked

6 tablespoons coffee beans

1 cup shallots, thinly sliced

2 tablespoons butter

3 tablespoons honey

1 cup sugar

1 cup Xérès sherry vinegar

1½ tablespoons kosher salt

»

PREPARE VENISON FILLING

Dice venison and fatback into small cubes and place on a tray lined with parchment paper. Let rest in freezer until semifrozen.

In a small bowl, mix together salt, sugar, garlic, pimiento and powders. In a second small bowl, combine red wine, vinegar and water. Keep very cold.

Chill grinder's attachment, blade and mixing bowl. Grind venison and pork cubes into the very cold mixing bowl.

Fit grinder with the paddle attachment and mix spices and meat on slow speed. When spices are incorporated, turn mixer to medium and slowly pour in wine mixture. Keep mixing for 30 to 60 seconds, until tacky. Pinch off a small amount and cook a tester, tasting for seasoning. Adjust as needed. Keep cold until ready to pipe.

Load meat into chamber of stuffer, pushing down to remove as many air pockets as possible. Wet nozzle of stuffer and slide casings on the end. Tie end of casing and hold with one hand as you turn on machine and meat feeds into casing. The casing will automatically come away from the feeder tube, so just hold sausage to guide the process. Tie sausages off into 3-ounce lengths, about 5 inches long. Gently pinch the meat and twist the casing to form logs. Using a sharp knife, cut through the middle of the twisted casing. Chill sausage until ready to cook.

PREPARE GASTRIQUE

Melt butter over medium-high heat, stirring, until light brown. Add peppercorns and coffee beans and toast over low heat, stirring constantly, until mixture becomes fragrant.

Add shallots and cook for another 2 minutes while stirring.

Add honey, sugar, vinegar and salt. Reduce until mixture glazes a chilled plate. Strain and adjust seasoning as needed.

PREPARE VINAIGRETTE

Place vinegar and mustard in a small bowl and slowly whisk in oils.

PREPARE APPLE–COCOA NIB SALAD

On a Japanese mandoline with the large-tooth blade, shave apple into a bowl. Fit mandoline with the flat blade and shave turnips into ¼-inch-thick pieces. Combine with frisée, shallot and cocoa nibs and coat with cider vinaigrette. Season to taste.

ASSEMBLE

Gently poach sausages in water until internal temperature reaches 135°F. Mark on a grill to char the outside.

Slice sausage and place on plate. In quick and steady fashion, use a spoon to swirl 1 tablespoon gastrique around edge of plate. Plate salad so it leans against sausage. Serve immediately.

CIDER VINAIGRETTE

¼ cup cider vinegar, good-quality brand

1 tablespoon Dijon mustard

⅔ cup extra-virgin olive oil

2 tablespoons pistachio oil

APPLE–COCOA NIB SALAD

½ apple, such as Fuji, Gala, Pink Lady, etc.

2 small turnips, preferably Tokyo

1 cup frisée, white parts only, rinsed and spun dry

⅛ cup shallot, finely diced

⅛ cup cocoa nibs, toasted and cooled

Kosher salt and freshly ground black pepper

In Dunnellon, Florida, outside Ocala, Seely's Ark farm produces fresh rabbit for us to use year-round. If you're squeamish about using rabbit, you can easily substitute chicken, guinea hen or pheasant. In the summer months, we substitute nectarines or peaches for the apples. The outcome is equally delicious. And if you want to substitute store-bought chutney for the recipe below, that's OK, too.

OCALA RABBIT BRATWURST

WITH FUYU PERSIMMON CHUTNEY AND QUINCE CARAMEL

SERVES 8 TO 10

RABBIT BRATWURST

1 pound rabbit meat, diced small

½ pound Pancetta Tesa (page 123) or pork belly

1 ounce sage leaves, minced

1 Honeycrisp apple, diced

½ teaspoon mace, ground or powdered

½ teaspoon yellow mustard powder

¼ teaspoon cayenne powder

4 garlic cloves, whole

¼ cup nonfat milk powder

⅓ ounce kosher salt

Freshly ground black pepper

Hog casings, soaked overnight in water

FUYU PERSIMMON CHUTNEY

Makes 18 ounces, can be jarred

1 tablespoon grapeseed oil

¼ cup yellow onion, finely diced

¼ cup shallots, finely diced

1 tablespoon brown mustard seeds

¼ cup dry sherry wine

5 ripe Fuyu persimmons, peeled

½ cup Xérès sherry vinegar

½ cup water

¼ cup golden raisins

½ cinnamon stick

Pinch of kosher salt

PREPARE RABBIT BRATWURST

Place rabbit and pancetta in a stainless steel bowl and freeze until firm but not solid. Add remaining ingredients to bowl and mix. Keep very cold.

Using a very cold meat grinder, grind all ingredients through the small die into a stainless steel bowl placed inside a bowl of ice. Divide mixture in half and grind one half a second time.

Place both meat mixtures in the bowl of a standing mixer fitted with the paddle attachment and whip on high for 45 seconds. Fry a small piece of the mixture to taste for seasoning. Adjust as needed; sausage should be highly seasoned.

Keep very cold until ready to pipe. Load meat into chamber of stuffer, pushing down to remove as many air pockets as possible. Wet nozzle of stuffer and slide casings on the end. Tie end of casing and hold with one hand as you turn on machine and meat feeds into casing. The casing will automatically come away from the feeder tube, so just hold sausage to guide the process. Tie sausages off into 2¼-ounce links, about 4 inches long. Gently pinch meat and twist casing to form logs. Using a sharp knife, cut through the middle of the twisted casing. Chill sausage until ready to poach.

PREPARE PERSIMMON CHUTNEY

Place oil in a sauté pan over medium-low heat. Add onion and shallots and sweat until translucent.

Increase heat to medium and add mustard seeds. Stir mixture continuously until seeds are slightly toasted and fragrant but without browning onion-shallot mixture.

Deglaze with sherry wine and cook until au sec.

Add persimmons, sherry vinegar, water, raisins, cinnamon stick and salt. Simmer until au sec. Let cool.

PREPARE QUINCE CARAMEL

Bring sugar and water to a boil over medium-high heat. Watching very closely, heat until sugar turns a nutty brown, 5 to 7 minutes.

Before caramel turns too dark and burns, carefully add quince and cook until very soft and falling apart, about 10 minutes.

Transfer to blender and puree until smooth. Refrigerate until ready to use.

ASSEMBLE

Place bratwurst in a pot and barely cover with cold water. Gently heat until internal temperature reaches 145°F.

Drain sausage and place in a large sauté pan over medium heat. Brown sausage in a little butter to give color to the casings. Let rest for 2 minutes before slicing.

Smear caramel on each plate. Place a nice quenelle of chutney on top of caramel. Place warm sliced bratwurst beside chutney.

QUINCE CARAMEL

¼ cup sugar

2 tablespoons water

2 pineapple quince, peeled, cored and thinly sliced

1 teaspoon kosher salt

This is an elegant way to serve up the humble chicken liver. Here we prepare it to be served when cherries are at their summer peak, but you can easily substitute any season's fruit offerings.

POTTED CHICKEN LIVER
WITH CHERRY GELÉE AND APRICOTS

SERVES 8

POTTED CHICKEN LIVER

6 ounces pancetta or bacon, diced

2 pounds chicken livers, patted dry

Kosher salt and freshly ground black pepper

6 tablespoons butter

4 medium shallots, thinly sliced (about 1 cup)

8 garlic cloves, thinly sliced

8 sage leaves

1 cup port

¾ teaspoon Sel Rose No. 1

¼ cup crème fraîche

CHERRY GELÉE

⅓ cup port

2 tablespoons red wine vinegar

⅓ cup water

⅓ cup sugar

1 tablespoon kosher salt

10 ounces bing cherries, stemmed and pitted (about 2 cups)

1 gelatin sheet or 1 teaspoon unflavored powdered gelatin

GARLIC CROSTINI

1 loaf country bread, sliced

Extra-virgin olive oil or duck fat

Garlic cloves

FOR ASSEMBLY

8 apricots, cut into thin wedges

Extra-virgin olive oil

PREPARE LIVERS

Place pancetta in a large sauté pan over medium-low heat and render until slightly crisped. Using a slotted spoon, remove from pan, place in a medium bowl and keep pan hot.

Season livers with salt and pepper. Increase heat to medium and add livers to pan drippings. Sear on both sides and cook to medium-rare. Remove from pan with slotted spoon and add to reserved pancetta.

Reduce heat to low. Add butter to pan and swirl until melted. Add shallots, garlic and sage and cook slowly, stirring occasionally, until softened.

Increase heat to medium-high. Deglaze pan with port, scraping all browned bits from bottom of pan. Reduce until almost dry, lowering heat as needed. Cool slightly and then transfer to a food processor or blender. Add pancetta, livers and their juices. Sprinkle with Sel Rose and process until smooth, occasionally scraping down sides of bowl. Transfer to a large mixing bowl.

Whip crème fraîche until stiff peaks form, then fold into liver mixture. Adjust seasonings as needed and pack tightly into eight 4-ounce jars, leaving room for cherry gelée. Refrigerate until set.

PREPARE GELÉE

In a small saucepan, combine port, vinegar, water, sugar and salt. Bring to a simmer, stirring occasionally to dissolve sugar and salt. Place cherries in a small bowl and cover with heated liquid. Refrigerate overnight.

USING SHEET GELATIN:
Strain liquid into a small saucepan and gently heat. Soften gelatin sheet in cold water and squeeze dry. Add to heated liquid and stir to dissolve. Add gelée to chilled jars of potted liver and refrigerate until set.

USING POWDERED GELATIN:
Strain liquid from cherries and divide, placing ¼ cup in a small bowl and remainder in a small saucepan. Gently heat liquid in saucepan. Sprinkle powdered gelatin over liquid in bowl and allow to soften for 1 minute. Stir warmed liquid into softened gelatin. Add gelée to chilled jars of potted liver and refrigerate until set.

(**NOTE** Cherries may be reserved for another use.)

PREPARE CROSTINI

Slice bread and brush with oil or duck fat. Grill and rub warm bread with garlic cloves.

ASSEMBLE

Toss apricots with just enough oil to make them shine and place on top of jarred potted liver and cherry gelee. Serve with garlic crostini and freshly ground black pepper.

This terrine is, more accurately, a roulade. We came up with it when we had lots of duck gizzard confit and lardo (cured fatback) trim that were only good enough for dicing. We decided to use a standard terrine recipe for the farci of primarily duck meat, and fold in the trim of gizzards and diced lardo. For visual and excessive aesthetics, we rolled the farci in "shingled" lardo for a circular border to the terrine.

TERRINE OF DUCK GIZZARD CONFIT AND LARDO

MAKES 16 SLICES

DUCK GIZZARD CONFIT

1 tablespoon kosher salt

½ teaspoon sugar

¼ teaspoon freshly ground black pepper

3 ounces duck gizzards

Duck fat (about 2 cups)

TERRINE

⅓ cup port

3 tablespoons brandy

⅓ cup shallots, thinly sliced

2 garlic cloves, thinly sliced

½ cup onion, thinly sliced

1 teaspoon sugar

2 bay leaves

¼ cup thyme, stems removed

½ teaspoon finely ground white pepper

3 ounces fatback, diced ¼ inch

3 ounces duck gizzard confit, diced

3 ounces duck or chicken liver

1 pound duck breast, diced

¼ pound pork shoulder, diced

2 teaspoons kosher salt

1 teaspoon Sel Rose No. 1

1 egg

1 pound lardo, thinly shaved (bacon or prosciutto can easily be substituted)

1 cup Activa RM

PREPARE CONFIT

Mix salt, sugar and pepper and coat gizzards with mixture. Place in a plastic container and refrigerate for 24 hours.

The next day, rinse gizzards under cold water. Let sit at room temperature for 1 hour.

Preheat oven to 225°F.

Place gizzards in a small casserole dish. Warm enough duck fat to cover them. Cover dish with foil. Cook for 1 hour, or until gizzards are tender. Let gizzards rest in fat for at least 6 hours in refrigerator.

Remove from refrigerator. Gently warm dish until fat liquefies. Remove gizzards and dice into ¼-inch pieces. Strain fat and reserve for another use.

PREPARE TERRINE

Place port, brandy, shallots, garlic, onion, sugar, bay leaves, thyme and pepper in a medium pot over medium-high heat. Reduce until liquid has evaporated. Remove from heat, remove bay leaves and refrigerate for 30 minutes.

Chill the grinder attachments (medium die), a bowl, fatback and duck gizzard confit for 30 minutes.

Combine shallot mixture with liver, duck breast, pork shoulder, salt, Sel Rose and egg, mixing well.

Grind liver mixture into chilled bowl using medium die. Gently fold in fatback and gizzards. Poach a small piece in a very small amount of water, tasting for seasoning. Adjust as needed. Refrigerate mixture until very cold.

Set a large pot of water over low heat, attach a thermometer and bring to 145°F.

Place a large piece of plastic wrap on counter. Set duck mixture in center and form a log, wrapping and twisting ends to create a tight roll. Using a toothpick, pop any air bubbles that form.

»

On a cookie sheet, shingle lardo slices in overlapping layers the length of the wrapped duck mixture. Sprinkle Activa over lardo. Unwrap duck mixture, being careful to preserve its cylindrical shape. Roll log onto lardo until completely covered.

Transfer shingled log to clean plastic wrap, roll firmly and seal ends with butcher's twine.

Place in the warm water for about 2 hours, depending on thickness of the log, until the internal temperature reaches 141°F. If you pierce the plastic wrap with the thermometer and have to add the terrine back to the water for further cooking, be sure to rewrap in new plastic wrap.

Place in an ice water bath for 20 minutes, then refrigerate for 24 hours.

ASSEMBLE

Unwrap terrine, slice into ½-inch disks and divide among plates. Garnish with assorted pickles and mustards.

FOR ASSEMBLY

Assorted pickles and mustards

SEAFOOD

SEVENTH COURSE

It's no secret: I love fish. Love to catch 'em, clean 'em, cook 'em, eat 'em and talk for days on end about them. When it comes to seafood, Florida is in the sweet spot. We talk with our fishmongers on a daily basis and our menus revolve around their freshest products. It's a great thrill to go to work and see what the day's catch will bring.

This dish is relatively easy to make and offers a stunning presentation. Keys to its success: use thin-skinned Meyer lemons and avoid the white pith, which turns the relish bitter.

GROUPER BAKED ON FIG LEAF
WITH BRUSSELS SPROUTS AND MEYER LEMON RELISH

SERVES 8

MEYER LEMON RELISH

- ¼ cup champagne vinegar
- 3 ounces shallots, sliced paper thin (about 1 cup)
- ¼ teaspoon sugar
- 3 Meyer lemons, quartered lengthwise, sliced paper thin, ends removed (about 2 cups)
- ⅓ cup extra-virgin olive oil
- 1½ teaspoons kosher salt

BRUSSELS SPROUTS

- ½ cup bacon or duck fat
- 2 pounds Brussels sprouts, sliced in half
- 12 ounces dried Mission figs, sliced in half and soaked in hot water for 20 minutes
- 1 cup Glazed Soffrito (page 214)
- 1 cup Chicken Stock (page 212)
- 2 tablespoons butter
- Kosher salt and freshly ground black pepper

FOR ASSEMBLY

- 8 large fig leaves, rinsed and covered with a damp towel to keep from drying
- 8 (6-ounce) grouper fillets
- Kosher salt and freshly ground black pepper

PREPARE RELISH

Place shallots and sugar in a medium bowl and cover with vinegar. Add lemon, oil and salt. Let rest for 45 minutes to meld flavors. Relish can be refrigerated in an airtight container for up to 5 days.

PREPARE BRUSSELS SPROUTS

Heat fat in a large sauté pan until lightly smoking. Add Brussels sprouts and brown quickly. Add figs, soffrito, stock and butter. Toss until emulsified and season to taste. (Brussels sprouts do not need to be cooked through because they will finish with the grouper.)

ASSEMBLE

Preheat oven to 400°F.

Lay fig leaves on an oiled sheet pan and top with Brussels sprouts. Season grouper to taste and place fillets on fig leaves. (Be sure to center them so leaves can curl around fish.) Bake for 7 to 8 minutes, until cooked through. Plate and top with relish.

VINCE LUISE

WE LUCKED OUT WHEN OUR FRIENDS at Gary's Seafood hooked us up with Vince Luise, ace spearfisherman and the guy who hauls in some of our finest flounder, grouper, cobia and snapper.

After spending years as a landscaper, Vince decided to go into business for himself doing what he loves best. Now he loads up his boat with scuba gear three or four days each week and heads out from Ponce Inlet or Port Canaveral, diving anywhere from 15 to 60 miles offshore at depths of up to 160 feet. It's not uncommon for Vince to spear up to 200 pounds of southern flounder on a single dive. And let's just say he tries not to think about sharks on the way back up to the surface.

Spearfishing as practiced by Vince can be a more sustainable way of harvesting fish. Unlike some commercial fishermen, Vince is able to target exactly what he's after without killing unwanted species in a bycatch.

"We never overfish our favorite spots," says Vince. "We know that's our bread and butter out there, and we have to make sure it keeps producing for us."

Mechanix

When working with awesome fresh flounder like we get from Vince Luise, you want to let the fish stand out on its own. Here it's the star with some great supporting actors.

FLOUNDER

WITH CORN, ONION FONDUE, FARRO AND EGGPLANT AGRODOLCE

SERVES 8

SWEET ONION FONDUE

5 tablespoons butter

1½ pounds sweet onions, peeled and sliced paper thin (about 4 cups)

½ teaspoon sugar

1 teaspoon kosher salt

1 bay leaf

Cheesecloth sachet of 2 sprigs fresh thyme

FARRO

2 tablespoons butter

1 cup farro

3 cups Chicken Stock (page 212), chilled

1 teaspoon kosher salt

FLOUNDER

8 (6-ounce) flounder fillets

Kosher salt and freshly ground black pepper

½ cup grapeseed or canola oil

FOR ASSEMBLY

1 cup corn cut from cob

3 tablespoons fines herbes

Kosher salt and freshly ground black pepper

1 cup Eggplant Agrodolce (page 215)

PREPARE FONDUE

Melt butter in a large saucepan over very low heat. Add onions, sugar, salt, bay leaf and sachet. Cover with parchment that has a small cutout in the center to ventilate (a cartouche). Simmer over lowest possible heat for 2½ hours. Remove bay leaf and sachet and discard. Refrigerate until ready to use.

PREPARE FARRO

Melt butter in a medium saucepot. Add farro and toast, stirring, 4 to 5 minutes. Pour cold stock over farro, add salt and bring to a boil. Lower heat and let simmer for 45 minutes. Remove from heat and drain any excess juices. Pour farro onto a sheet pan to halt cooking, and let cool.

PREPARE FLOUNDER

Pat flounder dry and season to taste. Place oil in a large sauté pan over medium-high heat. When oil is dancing, add fillets to pan. Don't flip until fish is 90 percent cooked. Then flip and remove from heat to finish cooking.

ASSEMBLE

Heat onion fondue, farro and corn in a medium pan. Bring to a simmer, add fines herbes and adjust seasoning as needed.

Divide farro mixture among 8 plates and top each with a flounder fillet. Garnish with a spoonful of eggplant and additional fines herbes.

When I was a kid, my father would take me reef fishing at night in the Florida Keys. Dad kept me busy pestering snapper with shrimp and cut-up squid while he was at the other end of the boat trying to catch bigger things. The yellowtails stole my bait at least half the time, but I finally got good enough to know the exact timing of their nibble and when to set the hook. Dad had to start giving me a "bag limit" because I was too young to use a fillet knife and he got stuck cleaning them all. At the restaurant, one of my favorite chores is butchering fish, and it always makes me think of those days spent fishing with Dad.

YELLOWTAIL SNAPPER
WITH POLENTA, ARUGULA PESTO AND PEPERONATA

SERVES 8

PREPARE PEPERONATA

Preheat oven to 400°F.

Rub peppers in 2 tablespoons oil and place on a cookie sheet. Roast for 30 minutes or until skins have darkened and blistered.

Place peppers in a large bowl and cover with plastic wrap to steam for 10 minutes.

Peel off pepper skins, discard seeds and julienne. Place basil sprigs in a large bowl.

Sweat shallots and garlic in 2 tablespoons oil over medium-high heat for 1 minute or until soft. Add peppers and bring to a simmer. Remove from heat and pour over the basil. Add vinegar and remaining oil, then season to taste. Can be used immediately but will be more flavorful if made ahead.

PREPARE PESTO

Blanch arugula and basil in boiling salted water for 30 seconds. Drain and shock immediately in ice water. Drain and squeeze excess water from greens.

Place in a blender with oil and walnuts. Puree until starting to become smooth. Add Parmesan and garlic and season to taste. Puree for 10 seconds to just combine. Immediately chill in a bowl placed in an ice bath to preserve the green color.

PEPERONATA

1½ cups red bell peppers

1½ cups orange bell peppers

½ cup green bell peppers, or poblano or jalapeño chiles

1 cup extra-virgin olive oil

6 sprigs fresh basil

½ cup shallots, thinly sliced

¼ cup garlic, thinly sliced

½ cup Xérès sherry vinegar

Kosher salt and freshly ground black pepper

ARUGULA PESTO

4 ounces arugula

4 ounces basil leaves

1 cup extra-virgin olive oil

¼ cup walnuts, toasted

1 ounce Parmesan, Microplaned

5 garlic cloves, Microplaned

Kosher salt and freshly ground black pepper

POLENTA

2 cups whole milk

2 cups Chicken Stock (page 212)

Kosher salt

1 cup coarse polenta, preferably Anson Mills

YELLOWTAIL SNAPPER

8 (6-ounce) yellowtail snapper fillets, skin on, bones removed and scored

2 tablespoons kosher salt

¼ cup vegetable oil

1 stick (¼ pound) butter

8 sprigs fresh thyme

FOR ASSEMBLY

Small leaves arugula

Small leaves fresh basil

PREPARE POLENTA

Simmer milk, stock and salt in a large Dutch oven over medium heat. Slowly whisk in polenta and cook for 45 minutes, stirring often. Season to taste and keep warm.

PREPARE SNAPPER

Season fillets with salt. Place oil in a sauté pan over high heat. When oil is dancing, add snapper skin side down. Sauté until skin is golden brown and fish is 90 percent cooked. Flip fillets and add butter and thyme. Remove from heat to finish cooking.

ASSEMBLE

Mix pesto into polenta and divide among 8 plates. Place warm fish over polenta and top with peperonata. Garnish with arugula and basil leaves.

When pompano are biting, it makes you glad to be in Florida for the chance to enjoy this wonderful fish at its freshest. On rare occasions, we also get the larger African pompano. Full of flavor without being fishy, high in fat without being oily, pompano is a firm-flesh fish, yet it flakes at the touch of a fork. We like to use it in a play on an Italian fish stew, topped with a creamy aioli, a combination that has had many a variation throughout the years at Luma.

BRAISED POMPANO

WITH TANGERINE-FENNEL CIOPPINO, GREEN CHICKPEAS AND BASIL AIOLI

SERVES 8

TANGERINE-FENNEL CIOPPINO

1 small red onion, thinly sliced

1 large fennel bulb, thinly sliced

2 garlic cloves, thinly sliced

1 teaspoon sugar

2 teaspoons Aleppo pepper flakes or Espelette

¼ cup extra-virgin olive oil

2¼ cups Tomato Water (page 216)

1 cup plus 2 tablespoons freshly squeezed tangerine juice

1 cup clam juice, Chicken Stock (page 212) or Fish Stock (page 212)

1¼ cups fresh green chickpeas, cooked and warmed

Herb sachet with 5 sprigs fresh basil

POMPANO

¼ cup vegetable oil

8 (6-ounce) pompano fillets, skin on

FOR ASSEMBLY

Basil Aioli (page 215)

Small leaves fresh basil

PREPARE CIOPPINO

Sweat onion, fennel, garlic, sugar and pepper in oil for about 5 minutes over medium-high heat. Add tomato water, tangerine juice and stock. Simmer for 2 to 4 minutes.

Add chickpeas and heat through. Taste for seasoning and adjust as needed. Add sachet, remove pan from heat and transfer mixture to a baking dish.

PREPARE POMPANO

Preheat oven to 300°F.

Place oil in a sauté pan over medium-high heat. Sear fish, skin side down, until about halfway cooked. Place fish atop cioppino in the baking dish. Cover with foil and bake for 5 minutes. Remove basil sachet.

ASSEMBLE

Divide among 8 bowls. Add 2 tablespoons aioli to each bowl and garnish with basil leaves.

This is a great make-ahead, al fresco dish. With the sauce vierge already prepared, all you need to do is prepare the swordfish and Broccolini. We like to warm the sauce to generously garnish the top of the fish.

GRILLED SWORDFISH
WITH CHARRED BROCCOLINI AND ARTICHOKE SAUCE VIERGE

SERVES 8

ARTICHOKE SAUCE VIERGE

1 (8-ounce) jar grilled artichokes, preferably Iposea, drained and diced

½ cup Meyer Lemon Relish (page 137)

⅓ cup sun-dried tomatoes, drained and diced

⅔ cup olives, mixed varieties, drained and julienned

¼ cup caperberries or 1 tablespoon capers, sliced in half

1 tablespoon fines herbes

1 cup extra-virgin olive oil

Kosher salt and freshly ground black pepper

SWORDFISH WITH BROCCOLINI

1½ pounds Broccolini, large stems removed, cut 3 to 4 inches long

½ cup extra-virgin olive oil

8 (6-ounce) swordfish steaks

Kosher salt and freshly ground black pepper

PREPARE SAUCE VIERGE

Combine all ingredients and season to taste. Set near grill to keep warm.

PREPARE SWORDFISH

Preheat grill to medium-high.

Toss Broccolini with ¼ cup oil and season to taste. Without flaming or browning, grill until well colored. Transfer to a warm spot on the grill with no flame.

Baste swordfish in remaining oil. Lightly season, then grill each side for about 5 minutes, depending on thickness of steaks.

ASSEMBLE

Divide Broccolini among 8 plates. Lay swordfish steaks on top of the stalks. Spoon sauce vierge generously over swordfish.

CHOKOLOSKEE

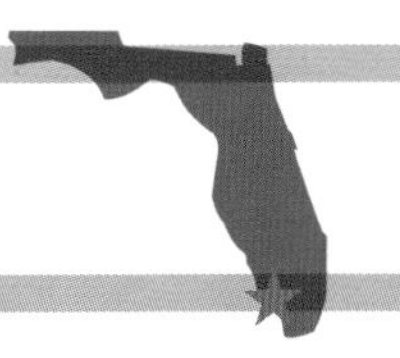

IF I'M NOT IN THE KITCHEN OR WITH MY FAMILY, there's a pretty good chance you'll find me fishing. I live and breathe fly-fishing for tarpon, snook or redfish. And one of my favorite places for escaping and relaxing is the Ten Thousand Islands, outside of Chokoloskee.

While these fishing trips might appear to be purely recreational, they are key to being a good chef. (At least that's what I keep telling my wife.) In the early 1990s, at the beginning of my cooking career, I landed a job in the kitchen at Stars in San Francisco, which was presided over by chef and owner Jeremiah Tower, one of the gods of California cuisine. Stars was crazy busy, unlike any restaurant I have ever seen. For new hires, it was baptism by fire, and they were assigned to the busiest of stations, just to see if they could handle the pressure.

One evening, working the hot-appetizers station, I was spinning in circles and accomplishing nothing when Chef Jeremiah approached me. In his trademark Cali–British accent, he said: "Young man, you must slow down, so you can speed up." He pushed me aside, stepped to the stove, made a couple of swift yet efficient moves and produced a beautifully finished dish.

There's not a day that goes by in our kitchens, in the midst of all the craziness, that I don't invoke the words of Chef Jeremiah. And it occurred to me early on that if I followed this mantra in all facets of life, then I might get more done.

That's why I go fishing every chance I get.

Just because we're out in the middle of the Ten Thousand Islands, miles and miles from civilization, doesn't mean that my fishing buddies and I have to dine on typical camping trip fare. We like to load up several coolers, head for a favorite spot like New Turkey Key and turn the beach into an outdoor kitchen that helps sustain us through long days on the water.

The beauty of the dishes that follow is that they can be prepped at home beforehand and then boated to base camp to be finished off over a small stove or open fire. Of course, eating well won't guarantee you catch fish, but it will certainly comfort you when you don't.

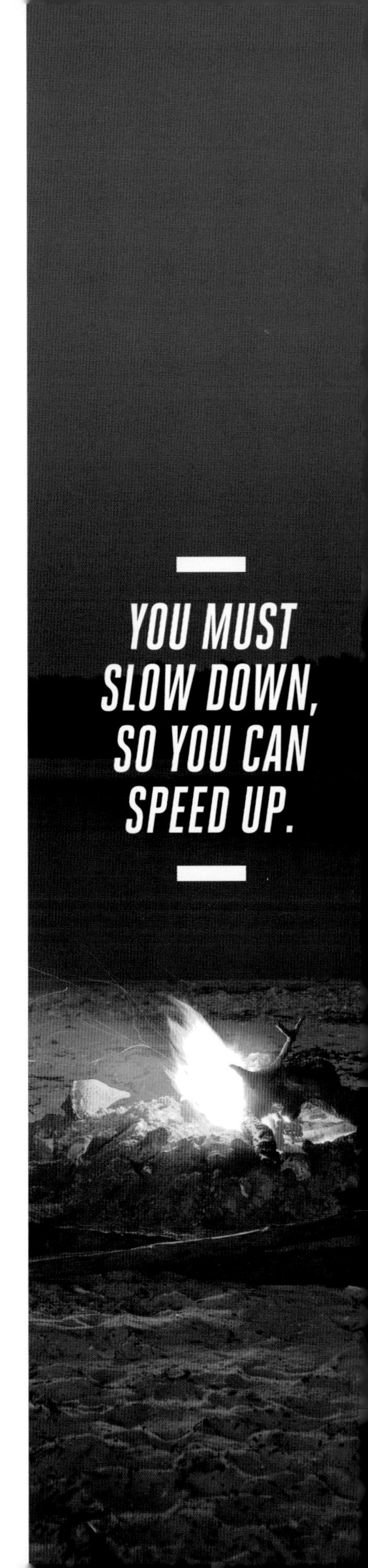

Over the years, the Ten Thousand Islands have offered refuge for countless numbers of people wanting to live outside the law, none more notorious than Ed Watson. Thought to have murdered more than a dozen men and women, many of whom he had hired to work on his sugar cane farm near Chatham Bend, Watson instilled fear in local folks for the two decades that he made his home in the Islands. Watson met his end one day in 1910 when he stepped off his boat near Ted Smallwood's store in Chokoloskee and was shot down by a group of local residents. This one goes out to them.

SMALLWOOD'S REVENGE

MAKES 1 COCKTAIL

INGREDIENTS

6–8 fresh mint leaves, torn into small pieces

1 tablespoon sour orange juice (or 1½ teaspoons orange juice plus 1½ teaspoons lime juice)

2 ounces Bulleit bourbon

4 ounces ginger beer

Crushed ice

METHOD

Place mint leaves in the bottom of a rocks glass, add orange juice and muddle. Add bourbon and ginger beer. Stir. Finish with crushed ice and garnish with more mint leaves.

When you are out in the middle of nowhere on a camping trip and hungry for fast food (it's OK to admit it), this satisfies the craving. It's all about the umami, baby.

HEARTS OF PALM
WITH KIMCHEE

SERVES 8

INGREDIENTS

1 cup kimchee

¼ cup freshly squeezed lime juice

1 tablespoon Korean chili powder or Sriracha sauce

Kosher salt

1 cup mayonnaise

2 pounds fresh hearts of palm, shaved lengthwise

METHOD

Place kimchee and its liquid in a blender with lime juice and spice. Puree for about 1 minute, then add mayonnaise and blend until smooth.

Add salt and adjust seasoning as needed. Toss mixture with hearts of palm about 20 minutes before serving.

These beans hold a special place in my heart. I cooked them for my sister's post-wedding brunch, which led to a conversation with a hungry and inquisitive woman named Liz, who later became my wife.

These beans don't really take all day to cook, but they do require soaking dried beans overnight, then cooking them and letting them sit in their cooking liquid for a second night. So they are technically 48-hour beans. They provide a base for our Badass Cassoulet (page 189) and are an essential part of family-style picnics.

ALL DAY BAKED BEANS

SERVES 10 TO 12

BEANS

- 2 cups dried beans (such as cannellini, haricot tarbais, black-eyed pea, Sea Island red pea or gigande beans), soaked overnight, drained and rinsed
- 8 cups cold water or Chicken Stock (page 212)
- 1 carrot, peeled
- 1 onion, peeled
- 1 celery stalk
- 1 bay leaf
- Herb sachet with fresh thyme and rosemary
- Kosher salt and freshly ground black pepper
- ½ cup extra-virgin olive oil or duck fat

FOR ASSEMBLY

- 1 pound Pancetta Tesa (page 123) or bacon, thickly sliced then cut in ½-inch pieces
- 1 medium tomato, diced
- ¼ cup tomato paste
- 2 cups Soffrito Crudo (page 214)
- 1 tablespoon arbol chili powder or Espelette
- 1 tablespoon fresh parsley, chopped
- 1 teaspoon fresh thyme leaves, chopped
- 1 teaspoon fresh sage leaves, chopped
- 6 cups Beans, plus their cooking liquid

PREPARE BEANS

Place beans in a pot and cover with water. Add carrot, onion, celery, bay leaf and sachet. Bring to a simmer. Skim and discard any impurities. Cook until beans are just tender, about 1 hour, depending on type of bean. Season lightly, add oil and refrigerate overnight.

ASSEMBLE

Preheat oven to 250°F.

Place pancetta in a roasting pan over medium heat on stovetop. Stirring frequently, cook pancetta until crispy, about 15 minutes. Add tomato and tomato paste, stirring to prevent over-browning, about 4 minutes. Add soffrito, chili powder and herbs and cook for 2 minutes. Add beans and their cooking liquid, stirring well to deglaze the pan and incorporate into other ingredients. Transfer roasting pan to oven and bake for 4 hours. Check frequently, adding liquid as needed and stirring caramelized top back into beans to give a deeper, richer flavor. Remove from oven. Adjust seasoning and spices as needed. Let cool before storing; beans can be saved for up to 4 days.

When you work at a restaurant, you often learn more from your colleagues in the kitchen than you ever did at culinary school. These are the best collard greens I've ever eaten, and I thank Bert Chapman for teaching me how to make them when we worked together at Bacchanalia in Atlanta.

CHAPPIE'S COLLARDS

SERVES 8 TO 10

INGREDIENTS

⅓ cup grapeseed oil

1½ pounds bacon lardons

4 cups diced onions (about 1½ pounds)

⅓ cup thinly sliced garlic (about 9 cloves)

1 tablespoon arbol chili powder

4 pounds collard greens, stemmed and cut crosswise into thin ribbons (turnip greens may be substituted)

2 sticks (½ pound) unsalted butter

¼ cup molasses

2 cups Xérès sherry vinegar

2 cups agave nectar

8 cups apple cider

8 cups Chicken Stock (page 212)

2 teaspoons kosher salt

METHOD

Place oil and bacon in a large stockpot over medium-low heat and render until very crispy. Add onion, garlic and chili powder and cook until softened. Add greens, toss and cook briefly until limp. Add butter, stirring until melted. Stir in remaining ingredients and bring to a simmer. Cook for 2 to 3 hours, until liquid is slightly reduced.

NOTE If too sweet, add a splash more of vinegar, or season with additional chili powder as needed.

Don't even think about making this dish with instant grits. Yes, stone-ground grits take longer to prepare, but it is definitely time well spent.

GOAT CHEESE GRITS

SERVES 8

INGREDIENTS

1 cup coarse, stone-ground grits (such as Anson Mills)

2½ cups milk

1 tablespoon butter

6 ounces goat cheese

Kosher salt and freshly ground black pepper

METHOD

Place grits, milk and butter in a heavy-bottomed saucepan and bring to a simmer. Stirring frequently, cook over very low heat for 1 hour or until thick and creamy and the "hard-grit bite" is gone. Fold in goat cheese and season to taste.

When camping in the Ten Thousand Islands, you're often awakened early in the morning by stone-crab fishermen heading out to pull their traps. Stone crabs are typically sold precooked, so you need to do little more here than heat them through.

STONE CRABS
WITH CURRY BUTTER AND BEER

SERVES 8

INGREDIENTS

8 pounds large stone crabs, cracked, shelled, slightly rinsed and patted dry (reserve knuckles for another use)

1 stick (¼ pound) unsalted butter, room temperature, divided

1 teaspoon hot curry powder

1 teaspoon sweet curry powder

1 cup beer (not hoppy, such as Stella Artois)

2 tablespoons heavy cream

¼ cup fresh parsley, stems removed

Fresh lemon juice

Kosher salt

METHOD

Place 1 tablespoon butter in a large sauté pan over medium heat. Add curries and toast slightly, 2 to 3 minutes. Deglaze pan with beer and let simmer for 1 minute. Add cream, reduce heat to low and slowly whisk in remaining butter. Once emulsified, add crab claws, mix to combine and warm gently over very low heat. Add parsley, then add lemon juice and salt to taste. Serve immediately.

Mustard is a natural emulsifier and helps the flour stick to the fish without eggs or milk. It also gives the fish a deep, tangy flavor. This method works well with shrimp, frog legs and chicken, too, but since I learned it on a fishing trip in the bayous of Louisiana, I will always fondly associate it with a long, productive day on the water.

MUSTARD BATTERED REDFISH
WITH KUMQUAT RÉMOULADE

SERVES 8 TO 10

KUMQUAT RÉMOULADE

- 8 kumquats, seeded and finely chopped, with their juices
- 1½ cups mayonnaise
- 1 tablespoon dill pickles, diced
- 1 tablespoon shallots, diced
- 1 tablespoon fresh parsley, chopped
- 1 teaspoon fresh tarragon, chopped
- 1 teaspoon lime juice
- 1 tablespoon orange juice
- Kosher salt and freshly ground black pepper to taste

MUSTARD BATTERED REDFISH

- Canola oil
- 1 cup yellow mustard (such as French's)
- ¼ cup water
- 1 tablespoon Tabasco sauce
- 2 cups flour
- Kosher salt and freshly ground black pepper
- 2 pounds redfish (or snapper or tripletail), skin off, pin bones removed, cut into 2-ounce portions
- Lime wedges

PREPARE RÉMOULADE

Combine all ingredients in a small bowl. Adjust seasoning as needed. Keep chilled until ready to serve.

PREPARE FISH

Fill frying pan with about 2 inches of oil and heat to 375°F. In a small bowl, mix mustard, water and Tabasco. In another small bowl, season flour. Working one piece at a time, dip fish in mustard mix, then dredge through flour, shaking to remove any excess. Drop fish into hot oil and repeat with more pieces, making sure not to overcrowd the pan. Cook until golden brown, flipping if necessary, about 5 minutes per piece. Drain on paper towels and adjust seasoning as needed. Serve with lime wedges.

Some homemade *mojo* and our Jerry Garcia Spice Blend bring zing to this Cuban classic.

PORK SHOULDER CUBANO

SERVES 8

INGREDIENTS

¼ cup lime juice

¼ cup lemon juice

½ cup orange juice

8 garlic cloves, minced

1 cup olive oil

1 cup Jerry Garcia Spice Blend (page 216)

1 (5-pound) pork shoulder, bone-in preferred

METHOD

Place juices, garlic, oil and spice blend in a blender. Puree until smooth. Place pork in a bowl, pour mojo sauce over it, cover and refrigerate overnight.

The next day, let rest at room temperature for 4 hours.

Preheat oven to 250°F.

Place pork fat-side up on the rack of a roasting pan. Cook for 8 to 9 hours, basting frequently with residual marinade and pan drippings. Don't rush it—pork is done when roast is dark brown and meat pulls away easily. Let rest, covered, at least 1 hour before slicing.

This is our nod to the classic key lime pie, not to mention the fact that it's a lot of fun eating dessert out of a jar.

KEY LIME POT DE CRÈME
WITH SUGAR CANE STREUSEL AND WHIPPED CRÈME FRAÎCHE

SERVES 8

SUGAR CANE STREUSEL

½ stick (¼ cup) unsalted butter, cubed

3 tablespoons sugar

2 tablespoons sugar cane syrup

⅓ cup all-purpose flour

¼ cup oats

KEY LIME POT DE CRÈME

5 cups heavy cream

4 tablespoons key lime zest (about 6 limes)

Vanilla bean split lengthwise, ½ reserved for another use

15 egg yolks

1 cup sugar

1 teaspoon salt

FOR SERVING

1 cup crème fraîche, whipped until light and fluffy

PREPARE STREUSEL

Preheat oven to 350°F. Line a sheet pan with parchment paper.

Place all ingredients in a bowl and blend with an electric mixer until well combined. Spread mixture thinly and evenly onto parchment-lined pan.

Bake until lightly browned, 10 to 12 minutes.

Cool and crumble into small pieces. Streusel can be made ahead and stored in an airtight container until ready to use.

PREPARE POT DE CRÈME

Combine cream, zest and vanilla bean in a medium saucepan and bring to a simmer. Remove from heat and allow mixture to steep for 1 hour.

Preheat oven to 325°F.

Whisk yolks, sugar and salt until light and pale in color. Return cream mixture to a simmer. Temper eggs by whisking a small amount of the heated cream into egg mixture. Add remaining cream and mix well.

Strain mixture using a fine-mesh sieve. Refrigerate for 4 hours or overnight.

Place eight 5-ounce jars or ramekins in a large baking dish and divide chilled mixture equally among them. Add enough hot water to come halfway up sides of jars. Cover baking dish tightly with foil and bake until custard is slightly set, 40 to 50 minutes.

Remove jars from water bath and refrigerate until chilled.

ASSEMBLE

Sprinkle pot de crème with sugar cane streusel and top each with a dollop of whipped crème fraîche.

ROASTS

EIGHTH COURSE

Contrary to popular belief, roasts are much better when served just slightly warm, not piping hot and straight from the oven. That's why they are the perfect choice for a dinner party. Roasts allow you to prepare ahead and then, when the guests arrive, you can cocktail it up, secure in the knowledge your main course is ready and resting, with the juices settling and keeping the meat tender and moist.

RULES FOR A GOOD ROAST

- Always temper your roast. Do not pull it from the refrigerator and put it directly into the oven. Let it come to room temperature over a couple of hours. This allows even distribution of heat and lets the meat cook evenly.
- High heat is not your buddy. Low and slow is the key. Anything over 350°F is overkill.
- Of poultry and pork—when in doubt, *brine!* It works wonders with shrimp and crab, too.
- Calibrate your oven periodically. Just like our loved ones, a little attention will keep it happy.

We like the clams from Cedar Creek Shellfish in New Smyrna Beach, which come from the waters of Florida's richest estuary—Mosquito Lagoon. Topped with quail, this is an elegant and hearty dish, but if you want to go with the chowder alone, then you won't feel shortchanged in the least.

BACON-WRAPPED QUAIL

WITH NEW SMYRNA BEACH CLAM CHOWDER

SERVES 4

CLAM CHOWDER

- 10 tablespoons (1¼ sticks) butter, divided
- 1 cup shallots, thinly sliced
- 3 fresh bay leaves
- 3 dozen clams, rinsed 3 times, purged in corn meal and rinsed once more
- 1 (750-milliliter) bottle dry white wine
- 1 large onion, sliced
- 1 large carrot, peeled and chopped
- 2 ribs celery, chopped
- ½ jalapeño, seeds and pith removed, sliced
- 1 garlic clove, split crosswise
- 1 bulb fennel
- 1 tablespoon kosher salt
- 1 cup heavy cream
- 1 cup half-and-half
- 2 tablespoons fennel seed
- 1 tablespoon black peppercorns

QUAIL

- 8 boneless quail (no ribcage or backbone)
- 4 tablespoons Compound Butter (page 214)
- 24 thin slices smoked bacon
- Grapeseed or canola oil

»

PREPARE CLAM CHOWDER

Using a pan large enough to hold clams in a single layer, melt 2 tablespoons butter, add shallots and bay leaves and cook until shallots soften. Add clams and white wine. Cover and steam until all clams have opened.

Strain, reserving liquid. When cool enough to handle, pick clams from shells. Discard shells, shallots and bay leaves. Pass clam broth through 4 layers of damp cheesecloth to remove any undesired particles. Repeat as needed. Set aside. Keep clams moist with a little broth and set remaining aside.

Melt remaining butter in a large saucepan over medium heat. Add onion, carrot, celery, jalapeño, garlic and fennel and cook. Do not allow to color. Add salt, clam broth, heavy cream and half-and-half and bring to a simmer.

Meanwhile, in a small saucepan over high heat, toast fennel seed and peppercorns, shaking constantly. When hot, toasted and aromatic, add to the simmering cream mixture to get a "spicexplosion" and simmer for another 3 minutes. Season to taste but be careful with the salt.

Strain through a chinois, pressing on solids to extract all liquid.

Keep chilled until ready to use.

PREPARE QUAIL

Remove thighbones and trim wing tips. Pipe 1½ teaspoons butter between skin and breast meat of each quail. Tuck and roll into natural form, crossing quail legs and securing by inserting one leg through a small slit cut in the other leg.

On a work surface, slightly overlap 3 bacon slices to create a shingle effect. Place quail breast side down at one end of the bacon shingle with legs and wings sticking straight. Roll so both ends of bacon finish on the same side of the quail. Repeat with remaining quail.

Chill well before cooking.

Remove quail from refrigerator. Place light layer of oil in a large sauté pan over high heat. When oil begins dancing, add cold quail seam side down, sliding to keep it from sticking.

Lower heat just enough to retain a slight sizzle. If bacon starts to curl you're cooking too fast. Flip quail when they start to brown and bond. Basting with oil, cook quail until golden brown, about 10 minutes. Transfer to paper towels and let rest.

ASSEMBLE

Melt butter in a large saucepan, add sliced garlic and cook for 1 minute. Add 3½ to 4 cups chowder to saucepan. Bring to a simmer and add soffrito, potatoes and chard. Stir until potatoes are heated through and chard is tender. Add clams, a squeeze of lemon and the parsley.

Divide chowder among bowls. Top with quail and garnish with celery leaves.

FOR ASSEMBLY

1 tablespoon butter

4 garlic cloves, thinly sliced

1 cup Yukon gold potatoes, diced and boiled

1 cup Glazed Soffrito (page 214)

1 cup fingerling potatoes, peeled, coined and boiled

1 cup Swiss chard, ribs removed, chopped in long strips, packed loosely

1 lemon, halved

⅛ cup parsley, chopped

½ cup celery leaves, chopped

Tiny seed clams from Cedar Creek Shellfish (above, left) ultimately produce succulent results on the half-shell.

You'll need to start marinating the duck at least two days before you plan to serve this dish, but the preparation is simple and there's a big payoff in flavor at the end. The tangerines provide a more intense citrus flavor, but it's fine to substitute oranges.

ROAST DUCK
WITH TANGERINE, STAR ANISE AND VANILLA

SERVES 4

INGREDIENTS

Zest of 2 tangerines
4 cups water
1 cup honey
8 star anise
2 cinnamon sticks
1 vanilla bean, split
4 cups tangerine juice
2 cups soy sauce
1 (4-to 5-pound) duck, giblets removed, rinsed
1 tangerine, halved

METHOD

In a large saucepan over medium-high heat, combine tangerine zest, water, honey, star anise, cinnamon sticks and vanilla bean and bring to a simmer. Stir in tangerine juice and soy sauce until well blended. Refrigerate until marinade is 42°F.

Transfer marinade to a large bowl. Submerge duck in marinade and refrigerate for 48 to 72 hours (the longer, the better).

Remove duck from marinade and bring to room temperature. Place half of the marinade in a saucepan and reduce until it's the consistency of a glaze, being sure to skim off any impurities that may rise to the surface.

Preheat oven to 250°F.

Insert a split tangerine inside duck cavity and place duck on the wire rack of a roasting pan. Roast for 2½ hours, glazing frequently, or until golden brown.

Allow duck to rest 30 minutes before carving.

BE THE ROADRUNNER

I WISH I COULD REMEMBER EXACTLY WHERE I first heard the expression "Be the roadrunner," so I could give proper credit. It is the number-one motto in our kitchens. We have "Be the roadrunner" signs posted on our bulletin boards to remind everyone that, just like Road Runner on that classic cartoon show, we should be swift and clever, bold enough to go right to the edge of the cliff without going over like poor ol' Wile E. Coyote.

It applies directly to the way we season our foods. Acids and salt, along with herbs and spices, are the kings of the kitchen. They put the pop in good food, take flavors to new heights, and we can't be shy about testing the limits. At the same time, we must recognize that if we overdo it, we'll wind up splattered on the canyon floor.

One of the key things to keep in mind when cooking is to season in layers. Add seasonings at various stages throughout a recipe, don't dump them all in at the end.

So, be the roadrunner. Beep-beep!

SPICE BLENDS

EXPERIMENTING WITH DIFFERENT SPICE BLENDS, we've come up with a few go-to favorites over the years. We like to give them names that speak to how we use them. There's Jerry Garcia, with its smoky, stony flavors; Gandhi, which throws Indian spices into the mix; and Pavarotti, which brings an Italian note to dishes. You can find the recipes in the Pantry section, starting on page 212.

One night early in my career, when I was working with a bunch of other young chefs at a big restaurant, we started playing "If I were on a deserted island and had only one bird to eat . . ." As the others called out duck or chicken, I yelled "Squab!" Yes, I chose pigeon.

Time has since taught me that ducks and chickens are far more versatile and would be the better choice for day-in, day-out dining. Still, I love squab. We like to air cure it in our Gandhi Spice for three to five days to intensify the flavors and help make the skin crispy. But take care not to overcook it or it will taste like something you don't want to eat, not even on a desert island.

AIR-CURED SQUAB

WITH LENTILS VINAIGRETTE AND BLOOD ORANGE MARMALADE

SERVES 8

SQUABS
(Must be made 3 to 5 days in advance)

8 squabs, livers and gizzards removed, patted dry

1 cup Gandhi Spice Blend (page 216)

½ cup canola or grapeseed oil

2 tablespoons kosher salt

4 tablespoons butter, melted for basting

BLOOD ORANGE MARMALADE

2 cups blood orange segments, membranes removed, juice reserved separately

1 Granny Smith apple, freshly grated

¼ cup shallots, minced

1 teaspoon fresh ginger, grated

3 tablespoons sugar

Zest of 2 oranges

½ teaspoon kosher salt

LENTILS VINAIGRETTE

½ cup fennel, diced ¼ inch

½ cup cucumber, diced ¼ inch, seeds removed

¼ cup red onion, diced ¼ inch

¼ cup mint, chiffonade

1 cup Sherry Vinaigrette (page 214)

3 tablespoons butter

1 cup Soffrito Crudo (page 214)

2 garlic cloves, minced

2 cups beluga lentils

4 cups water or Chicken Stock (page 212)

Kosher salt

PREPARE SQUABS

Rub spice blend all over each bird and place on a sheet pan that has been lined with a wire rack. Chill in refrigerator for 3 to 5 days, uncovered.

PREPARE MARMALADE

Combine blood orange juices, apple, shallots, ginger and sugar and reduce to consistency of light syrup. Add the segments and cook for 3 to 5 minutes. Remove from heat and fold in zest. Season with salt and chill for up to 1 week.

PREPARE LENTILS VINAIGRETTE

In a small bowl, combine fennel, cucumber, onion, mint and vinaigrette. Set aside.

In a large saucepot, sweat soffrito and garlic in butter for 2 to 3 minutes. Add lentils and stir for 1 to 2 minutes. Add stock and bring to a simmer. Cook until 90 percent of liquid has evaporated, 20 to 25 minutes. Remove from heat, cover and let rest for 10 minutes.

Remove lid and stir in the vinaigrette mixture. Season to taste.

FINISH SQUABS

Remove squabs from refrigerator and temper at least 1 hour.

Preheat oven to 300°F.

Place oil in a large sauté pan over medium-high heat. Season squabs with salt and sear on all sides until golden brown. Transfer to a roasting pan and place in oven. After 5 minutes, remove from oven to baste with butter. Return to oven until the internal breast temperature reaches 120°F, 5 to 8 minutes. Remove from oven, baste again and allow to rest for 10 minutes.

ASSEMBLE

Place a large spoonful of lentils vinaigrette on each plate. Remove legs and breasts from squabs and arrange upon the lentils. Top with blood orange marmalade.

Maybe I've had one too many gyros in my day, but whenever I think of lamb it's always a Greek/Mediterranean version. Here we marry the meat with the crunch of an Italian panzanella. The panzanella is delicious on its own but complements the lamb with grace, and the croutons are great for soaking up all the delicious lamb juices.

ROASTED LEG OF LAMB
WITH PANZANELLA "À LA GRECQUE"

SERVES 10 TO 12

LAMB MARINADE

½ cup Dijon mustard

¼ cup Greek yogurt

¼ cup garlic confit puree

2 tablespoons parsley, chopped

LAMB

1 (7- to 8-pound) leg of lamb, bone in

2 tablespoons kosher salt

2 teaspoons freshly ground black pepper

6 tablespoons canola or grapeseed oil

CROUTONS

½ cup extra-virgin olive oil

2 cups artisan-quality bread, cubed into ½-inch pieces

ANCHOVY AND BULGUR WHEAT PANZANELLA

2 cups pan juices from lamb

2 cups cucumbers, channeled, seeded, diced

⅓ cup oil cured olives

⅓ cup kalamata or Nicoise olives

⅓ cup gaeta or Castelvetrano olives

¼ cup red onion, julienned

3 to 4 heirloom tomatoes (about 2 cups), diced

8 ounces bulgur wheat, cooked

½ cup mint leaves, torn by hand

½ cup Italian parsley sprigs

½ cup basil leaves, torn by hand

1 cup Red Wine Vinaigrette (page 214)

2 cups reserved juices from roasted lamb, fat removed

16 white anchovies

Kosher salt and freshly ground black pepper

PREPARE MARINADE

Mix all ingredients well in a bowl. Set aside.

PREPARE LAMB

Rub lamb with salt and pepper, then douse with marinade. Place in a roasting pan and refrigerate, uncovered, for at least 24 hours. Remove 5 hours before serving time. Allow lamb to come to room temperature in marinade for 2 hours, then remove lamb and scrape off excess marinade into roasting pan. Set marinade aside.

Preheat oven to 375°F.

Pat lamb with paper towels. In a second roasting pan or large saucepan, heat oil on stovetop over medium-high heat. Add lamb and brown on all sides. Transfer to the original roasting pan and "remarry" the lamb with the marinade.

Bake for 10 minutes, or just until marinade is lightly browned, then lower to 275°F and cook until internal temperature reaches 120°F to 130°F, about 2½ hours. Let rest for 30 to 45 minutes, loosely covered (temperature will increase 5 degrees). Reserve cooking juices.

PREPARE CROUTONS

Heat oil in medium sauté pan over medium heat. Add bread cubes and sauté, stirring until golden brown. Drain on paper towels.

PREPARE PANZANELLA

In a bowl, add reserved cooking juices to the croutons and toss to absorb. Add remaining ingredients and mix well. Season to taste.

ASSEMBLE

Place panzanella on plates and top with slices of lamb.

Although not technically a roast, this is one of my favorite ways to cook beef for a party. Wrapping in plastic wrap is the first way that I learned sous vide, but use a vacuum pack machine instead if you have one. If you do not have a fancy immersion circulator, just monitor the water constantly to maintain as close to the poaching temperature of 138°F as possible. Keeping a separate pot of equal temperature water on the stove can help to regulate the temperature by adding more water if needed. Ask your butcher to prepare the ribeye minus the coulotte (or cap), leaving just the center cut eye of rib.

POACHED AND ROASTED PRIME RIBEYE FILLET

WITH ROASTED CARROTS, LA RATTE POTATOES AND RED WINE BÉARNAISE

SERVES 6 TO 8

RIBEYE

- 3 pound ribeye fillet, tied with butcher's twine
- 1 tablespoon kosher salt
- 2 teaspoons black pepper, cracked
- 4 tablespoons butter, room temperature
- 4 thyme sprigs
- 8 garlic cloves, sliced
- 3 tablespoons grapeseed or canola oil

ROASTED BABY CARROTS

- 1 pound baby heirloom carrots, tops trimmed
- 2 tablespoons grapeseed or canola oil
- 1½ teaspoons kosher salt
- 1 teaspoon sugar

ROASTED LA RATTE POTATOES

- 2 pounds La Ratte fingerling potatoes, cleaned and halved
- ¼ cup water
- 2 tablespoons extra-virgin olive oil
- 4 garlic cloves, halved
- 4 sprigs fresh thyme
- 1 tablespoon kosher salt
- 1 teaspoon freshly ground black pepper

PREPARE RIBEYE

Season beef with salt and pepper. Spread the butter around beef, and lay on the thyme and garlic. Wrap in plastic wrap about 10 times around and tie both ends with butcher's twine to seal. Place in 138°F water for 1 hour, spinning with tongs often to create movement. Remove and let rest for 20 minutes.

PREPARE CARROTS

Use a brand-new, medium-grade scouring pad under cool running water to remove excess dirt and skin from carrots. Dry on paper towels. Heat oil in a large sauté pan over high heat. Add carrots, caramelizing deeply. When almost finished, add salt and sugar. Keep warm until ready to serve.

PREPARE POTATOES

Preheat oven to 375°F.

Combine all ingredients in a shallow roasting pan and cover with foil. Roast for 25 to 30 minutes. Remove from oven when potatoes are easily pierced with a knife. Keep warm until ready to serve.

»

RED WINE BÉARNAISE (MAKES 2 CUPS)

¼ cup red wine

10 whole black peppercorns

1 sprig fresh thyme

1 bay leaf

4 garlic cloves

3 egg yolks, room temperature

8 tablespoons butter, room temperature

Kosher salt and freshly ground black pepper

PREPARE BÉARNAISE

In a small saucepan, combine wine, peppercorns, thyme, bay leaf and garlic. Cook until liquid is reduced by half. Remove from heat, strain out spices and, while hot, transfer liquid to a blender. Blend on high and quickly add yolks, 1 at a time. Next add butter, 1 tablespoon at a time. (If sauce becomes too thick add a touch of water). Season to taste and keep in a warm area to maintain temperature (not over heat) until ready to serve.

FINISH RIBEYE

Remove wrap from ribeye, reserving butter, thyme and garlic. Pat meat dry. Heat oil in a large sauté pan over medium-high heat until oil dances. Sear meat on all sides, browning deeply, 6 to 10 minutes. Lower heat. Add butter, thyme and garlic and baste for another 5 minutes. Remove from heat. Allow to rest 10 minutes before removing twine, then slice into 6 pieces.

ASSEMBLE

Place a ladleful of béarnaise on each plate and top with a slice of ribeye. Divide potatoes and carrots evenly and place next to meat.

PATZ & HALL
TE KOKO

AIR FLOW

I love clean bones poking out of beautifully roasted *(arrosto)* meat. This chop makes me feel like a Tuscan carnivore. The ramp gnocchi are not made with the traditional potato, but are still very Italian. The ramp greens can be easily substituted with another green such as Swiss chard, pea shoot or spinach.

VEAL RACK "ARROSTO"
WITH RAMP GREEN GNOCCHI AND RHUBARB CRUDO SALSA

SERVES 6

RHUBARB CRUDO SALSA

1¼ pounds rhubarb (about 2 cups), peeled (trimmings reserved), diced ¼ inch

1 cup red wine

1 cup water

1 cup sugar

1 tablespoon kosher salt

½ cup fennel (white parts), diced ¼ inch

1 cup Pickled Ramps (page 214), diced ¼ inch

½ cup extra-virgin olive oil

16 mint leaves, chiffonade

VEAL DRY RUB

4 tablespoons parsley, chopped

2 tablespoons thyme leaves, chopped

3 tablespoons kosher salt

1 tablespoon freshly ground black pepper

VEAL

5 pound veal rack (6 chops), chine bone removed, rib bones cleaned, tied

5 garlic cloves, sliced

6 sprigs fresh thyme

»

PREPARE SALSA

Place rhubarb trimmings in a medium saucepot and cover with wine, water and sugar. Bring to a simmer and cook for 10 minutes. Strain and chill liquid; set rhubarb aside. When liquid is cool, pour over rhubarb dice. Cover and refrigerate at least 12 hours. Mix in remaining ingredients to serve.

PREPARE DRY RUB AND VEAL

Mix parsley, thyme, salt and pepper. Pat dry rub mixture all over veal, and wrap in plastic. Refrigerate 6 to 8 hours.

COOK VEAL

About 3 hours before serving time, remove plastic and pat meat dry without removing spice rub. Allow veal to come to room temperature for at least 1 hour.

Preheat oven to 350°F.

Heat oil in a medium roasting pan on the stovetop. Sear roast, browning all sides. Add garlic and thyme and transfer to oven. Bake 60 to 70 minutes, until internal temperature reaches 125°F. Remove from oven and let rest for at least 30 minutes.

RAMP-RICOTTA GNOCCHI

2-3 cups ramp greens, loosely packed (spinach, chard or pea shoots can be substituted, enough to produce 5 tablespoons puree)

½ pound ricotta cheese, hung in cheesecloth sack overnight (about ⅔ cup drained)

1 egg white

1 egg

1 teaspoon kosher salt

¼ teaspoon freshly ground black pepper

3 tablespoons Parmesan cheese, grated

7 tablespoons premium 00 pasta flour

5½ tablespoons panko "fino" (panko crumbs pulverized in blender)

Olive oil

PREPARE RAMP-RICOTTA GNOCCHI

Prepare ramp-greens puree by blanching and shocking. In a blender, place greens and just enough cold water to get the mixture spinning. Puree until smooth. Mix puree, ricotta, egg white, whole egg, salt, pepper and Parmesan. Then fold in flour and panko, mixing well. Mixture should be stiff (if not, add a touch more panko). Bring pot of boiling salted water to a simmer, and with 2 spoons dipped in water (to prevent sticking), form a quenelle shape. Repeat until all dough is formed. Drop into salted boiling water. In small batches, cook for 3 minutes or until they float to the top. Use a slotted spoon to transfer to bowl. Toss with oil and cover loosely until ready to use.

ASSEMBLE

Slice veal rack in between each bone to make 6 servings. Sauté gnocchi in olive oil just to heat and place on plate next to veal chop. Top with salsa.

Our guests scream for this dish, and are rewarded upon the forecast of a rare cold front approaching the state of Florida. It only makes sense that we serve it on these uncommon nights when the air is crisper than the usual heat, although we sometimes we give in throughout our mild winter just to make folks happy.

BADASS CASSOULET

SERVES 12 TO 14

STANDARD CONFIT CURE

(We use the ratio of 1½ teaspoons of curing salt per pound of meat)

1 cup kosher salt

½ cup sugar

1 tablespoon freshly ground black pepper

CRISPY SKIN DUCK LEG CONFIT

8 duck legs

16 sprigs fresh thyme

8 garlic cloves, halved

10-14 cups duck fat (depending on cooking vessel; enough to cover duck legs completely)

DUCK GIZZARD CONFIT

1 pound duck gizzards (about 16)

4 sprigs fresh thyme

4 garlic cloves

2 cups duck fat

FOR ASSEMBLY

All Day Baked Beans (page 155)

3 tablespoons Sherry Vinaigrette (page 214)

1 cup Chicken Stock (page 212)

Venison Sausage (page 124) or Ocala Rabbit Bratwurst (page 126), halved lengthwise

2 tablespoons parsley, chopped

4 tablespoons Pangrattato (page 216)

PREPARE CONFIT CURE

Combine all ingredients in a bowl and set aside.

PREPARE DUCK LEG CONFIT

Sprinkle duck legs with confit cure and place in a bowl with thyme and garlic. Cover and refrigerate overnight. Remove excess seasoning, pat dry and let rest at room temperature for 2 hours.

Preheat oven to 225°F. Warm duck fat to 160°F. Place duck (skin side up), thyme and garlic in a small, deep roasting pan and submerge in duck fat. Cover with foil and bake for about 3 hours; the fat should have just a lazy bubble in it.

Using a slotted spatula, carefully check confit by removing 1 leg, placing on a plate and pushing tips of the bone towards each other. If they spring back, bake until bones offer no resistance when pushed, up to 5 hours. When done, let cool at room temperature for 1 to 2 hours, then use slotted spoon to transfer to sheet pan lined with parchment paper. Cover with plastic wrap and refrigerate overnight.

PREPARE DUCK GIZZARD CONFIT

Remove any excess fat from gizzards. Season with confit cure, thyme and garlic cloves and let sit in refrigerator for 3 hours. Rinse, pat dry, add gizzards to small casserole dish and cover with warm duck fat. Seal with foil and bake at 200°F for 1½ to 2½ hours, until easily pierced with a knife or toothpick. Let cool in fat overnight.

FINISH DUCK LEG CONFIT

When ready to serve, heat large non-stick pan over medium-high heat with ¼ inch duck fat. When fat is very hot and dancing, add duck legs to pan, skin side down. Lower heat to medium and cook for 15 minutes, basting with the fat, slowly rendering the fatty skin to crispy. When at desired crispness and browning (this is the best part and should not be taken lightly), flip legs and baste lightly, for less than 1 minute. Transfer to plate. Cool 1 to 2 minutes, skin side up. Gently twist the thighbone to remove, and discard.

ASSEMBLE

Warm beans and add vinaigrette and just enough stock to loosen mixture. Place bean mixture into bottom of 2½-quart baking dish. Layer sausage and gizzards next, firmly pressing into bean mixture so only tops remain above surface. Place duck confit on top.

Bake at 350°F for 20 to 30 minutes. When beans are bubbling, pull from oven and garnish with parsley and pangratatto.

SWEETS

NINTH COURSE

I was trained as a savory chef and don't have a background in desserts. Same thing for our amazing pastry chef Brian Cernell, who learned his craft on the job. But that's as it should be since desserts are a reflection of our overall cooking philosophy and we approach them just as we do savory foods. We are always looking for the perfect balance of textures, flavors and temperatures—whatever it takes to push this final course forward.

Curd: it's the new peanut butter. Well, that might be getting a little carried away, but curd is versatile and it can be made with all kinds of fruits—cherry, pineapple, passion fruit. If I could get away with putting curd on everything, I would. This is a good way to team it with some of our local citrus.

LEMON CURD

WITH SHORTBREAD COOKIES, TOASTED MERINGUE AND HUCKLEBERRY COULIS

SERVES 8 TO 10

LEMON CURD

6 large eggs

6 large egg yolks

1½ cups sugar

1 cup fresh lemon juice

½ cup lemon zest, grated

Pinch of kosher salt

2½ sheets gelatin, bloomed (or 1 packet Knox gelatin, bloomed in 4 tablespoons cold water)

8 tablespoons butter, softened, cut into pieces

SHORTBREAD COOKIES

1 pound butter (4 sticks), room temperature

1 cup powdered sugar

2 teaspoons vanilla paste

4 cups all-purpose flour

½ teaspoon kosher salt

HUCKLEBERRY COULIS

2 cups huckleberries, rinsed (blueberries can be substituted)

⅓ cup white sugar

Juice and zest of 1 large lemon

Pinch of kosher salt

»

PREPARE CURD

Whisk together eggs, egg yolks and sugar in a large bowl. Whisk in lemon juice, zest and salt.

In a double boiler over simmering water, gently cook and stir curd until thick enough to coat the back of a spoon, 7 to 10 minutes.

Remove curd from heat, add bloomed gelatin and whisk in butter. Press through a fine-mesh sieve.

Pour strained curd into 4-inch ring molds wrapped with plastic wrap. Immediately refrigerate and allow to set until firm, about 6 hours.

PREPARE SHORTBREAD COOKIES

Cream butter in a large bowl with an electric mixer. Add powdered sugar and mix until well combined. Mix in vanilla paste.

Place flour and salt in a separate bowl and whisk until well mixed.

Stream dry ingredients into butter-sugar mixture at medium-low speed until all ingredients are incorporated.

Remove dough from mixer, place on a sheet pan and flatten to about ½-inch thickness. Wrap tightly in plastic and refrigerate at least 4 hours.

Preheat oven to 350°F.

Remove dough from refrigerator, pound out slightly with flat side of a meat hammer or rolling pin and roll to ¼-inch thickness. Cut into 4-inch rounds.

Place cookies on a sheet pan lined with parchment paper. Bake for 8 to 10 minutes, until edges are lightly browned and centers are slightly soft.

Remove from oven and cool completely.

PREPARE COULIS

Combine all ingredients in a small saucepan. Cook over medium heat until sugar dissolves and berries begin to break down.

Continue cooking until juices begin to thicken slightly.

Place in a blender and puree until smooth. Pass through a fine-mesh sieve and allow to cool. (Use leftover coulis for sauce over ice cream.)

TOASTED MERINGUE

4 large egg whites, room temperature

1 cup white sugar

Juice and zest of 1 lime

PREPARE TOASTED MERINGUE

Place egg whites in a clean mixing bowl. Begin whipping on medium-high speed until whites are foamy and soft peaks begin to form.

Stream in sugar slowly until incorporated. Continue mixing, adding lime juice and zest. Increase speed to high and mix until firm peaks form.

ASSEMBLE

Place 1 cookie on each plate. Unmold lemon curds onto cookies. Pipe meringue on top of curd in a pyramid shape and lightly torch to toast. Drizzle coulis on plate.

On a visit to New York City, our pastry chef, Brian Cernell, and I met with legendary pastry chef Michael Laiskonis, when he worked at Le Bernardin. His work has been an inspiration to Brian, and this is a spin on one of Laiskonis's recipes for a soft ganache. It's fudgy without being too fudgy, and the tart cranberries play well against the rich chocolate.

CHOCOLATE GANACHE
WITH HAZELNUT CRUMBLE AND GRAND MARNIER–CRANBERRY SORBET

SERVES 8

GRAN MARNIER–CRANBERRY SORBET

2 cups water

1½ cups sugar

2½ cups cranberries

Zest of ½ large orange

½ teaspoon kosher salt

¼ teaspoon ground cinnamon

2 cups orange juice

¼ cup Grand Marnier

CHOCOLATE GANACHE

2½ cups heavy cream

11¼ ounces bittersweet chocolate (70 percent cocoa), chopped

¼ cup water

⅝ teaspoon flaked agar agar

1¼ teaspoons light corn syrup

Pinch of salt

¼ teaspoon gelatin, bloomed with 2 tablespoons cold water

HAZELNUT CRUMBLE

2 tablespoons butter, room temperature

¼ cup all-purpose flour

¼ cup white sugar

¼ cup dark brown sugar

¼ cup shelled hazelnuts, skinned, lightly toasted and crushed to ⅛ inch to ¼ inch in size

⅛ teaspoon salt

PREPARE SORBET

Combine water, sugar, cranberries, zest, salt and cinnamon in a medium saucepan. Bring to a boil, making sure cranberries have popped and sugar is fully dissolved. Cool and pour mixture into a container; cover and refrigerate overnight.

Puree mixture and strain through a fine-mesh sieve. Add orange juice and Grand Marnier, stirring well. Pour into an ice cream machine and run until mixture begins to firm up. Freeze for at least 2 hours or until firm.

PREPARE GANACHE

Place heavy cream in a saucepan and bring to a gentle boil. Place chocolate pieces in bowl. Pour cream over chocolate and stir until melted.

Place water, agar agar, corn syrup and salt in a 2-cup microwavable container; microwave on high for 2 minutes, stopping every 30 seconds to make sure ingredients are well mixed. Add to melted chocolate mixture. Add bloomed gelatin and stir until thoroughly incorporated.

Pour ¼ cup chocolate mixture into each of 8 small serving dishes. Cover and refrigerate at least 2 hours or until firm.

PREPARE CRUMBLE

Preheat oven to 350°F. Combine all ingredients in a medium bowl, mixing well to a crumble consistency.

Place on a parchment-lined sheet pan and bake until golden brown, 10 to 12 minutes. Cool and crumble into pebble-size pieces. Store in an airtight container until ready to serve.

ASSEMBLE

Remove ganache from refrigerator about 30 minutes before serving, or lightly torch bottom of each mold to soften slightly. Sprinkle about 2 tablespoons hazelnut crumble around side of each ganache. Shape sorbet into a quenelle and place on top of ganache. Serve immediately.

I love sweet corn and the idea of putting it into a dessert really appealed to me. We had a bunch of corncobs sitting around in the kitchen one day, so we steeped them in cream and made gelato out of that. Bing cherries come into season about the same time as sweet corn, so pairing the two made perfect sense.

SWEET CORN GELATO

WITH RICOTTA FRITTERS AND BING CHERRY COMPOTE

SERVES 6 TO 8

SWEET CORN GELATO

3 ears white or yellow sweet corn, kernels removed and reserved, cobs chopped into 1-inch pieces

4 cups milk

2 cups heavy cream

8 egg yolks

1 cup sugar

1 teaspoon kosher salt

BING CHERRY COMPOTE

2 cups Bing cherries, pitted

½ cup water

½ cup lemon juice

½ cup sugar

1 tablespoon brandy

½ teaspoon kosher salt

RICOTTA FRITTERS

½ cup all-purpose flour

¼ cup cake flour

2 teaspoons baking powder

2 tablespoons sugar

Zest of ½ lemon

Seeds from ¼ vanilla bean

1 cup ricotta

2 eggs

Canola or peanut oil

PREPARE GELATO

Combine corn kernels, cobs, milk and cream in a pot. Bring mixture to a simmer and remove from heat. Allow to sit for 1 hour.

Lightly puree corn mixture with a hand blender to break up some kernels. Strain mixture through a fine-mesh sieve. Place smooth mixture back in pot and bring to a simmer.

Combine yolks, sugar and salt in a large bowl and whisk until pale in color. Temper hot mixture into yolks, stirring constantly. Place mixture back on burner and continue cooking on low until it thickens or reaches 165°F.

Remove mixture from heat, pour into a bowl, cover and refrigerate overnight.

Strain mixture through fine-mesh sieve with hand blender to help mixture pass through. Place in an ice cream machine and spin until consistency of soft-serve ice cream. Transfer to an airtight container and freeze at least 1 hour.

PREPARE COMPOTE

Bring all ingredients to a boil in a saucepan. Reduce heat to a simmer and continue cooking until cherries soften and start to release juices, 10 to 12 minutes.

Remove cherries with a slotted spoon and transfer to a bowl. Continue cooking juices until thick enough to coat the back of a spoon. Pour juice over cherries and cool completely.

PREPARE RICOTTA FRITTERS

Whisk together both flours, baking powder and sugar in a mixing bowl. In a separate bowl, whisk together lemon zest, vanilla bean seeds, ricotta and eggs. Add wet ingredients to dry mixture; whisk to combine. Allow batter to rest for 30 minutes.

In a fryer or deep pot, heat oil to 365°F. Drop 1-tablespoon round scoops of batter into oil. Fry in small batches until fritters are golden brown, turning constantly for uniform cooking and color, about 3 to 5 minutes. Drain on paper towels and keep warm until all fritters are cooked.

ASSEMBLE

Place a scoop of gelato in a shallow bowl. Add 2 to 4 fritters, then drizzle cherry compote over gelato and fritters.

Our inspiration for this dessert was that beloved snack food—the Twinkie.

SOUR CREAM CAKE
WITH MACERATED RABBIT RUN FARM STRAWBERRIES

SERVES 8

SOUR CREAM CAKE

5 tablespoons unsalted butter, room temperature

1 cup sugar

1 cup sour cream

1 tablespoon vanilla paste

2 large eggs

1½ cups all-purpose flour

1 teaspoon baking powder

¼ teaspoon baking soda

½ teaspoon kosher salt

MACERATED STRAWBERRIES

1 quart Rabbit Run Farm strawberries, stemmed and quartered

3 tablespoons sugar

1 tablespoon lemon juice

WHIPPED SOUR CREAM

1 cup sour cream

1 teaspoon vanilla paste

2 tablespoons powdered sugar

PREPARE CAKE

Preheat oven to 350°F (325°F convection).

Place butter and sugar in the bowl of a mixer fitted with the paddle attachment. Cream mixture on medium speed until extremely light and fluffy.

Lower mixer speed to medium-low and add sour cream and vanilla. Mix until well combined. Add eggs, one at a time, scraping down sides of bowl in between each addition.

Sift together dry ingredients. Reduce mixer speed to low and add dry ingredients in 3 additions. Mix until just combined; do not overmix.

Grease and flour eight 4-ounce molds and place on a sheet pan. Divide batter among molds, smoothing surfaces slightly. Bake for 18 to 20 minutes, turning the pan halfway through, until toothpick inserted into center of cake comes out clean. When cool enough to handle, remove cakes from molds and continue cooling on a rack.

PREPARE STRAWBERRIES

Combine strawberries, sugar and lemon juice in a medium bowl and macerate at least 1 hour.

PREPARE SOUR CREAM

Place all ingredients in a small bowl and whisk until well combined.

ASSEMBLE

Place cakes on individual serving plates and top with strawberries and sour cream.

We love using a semifreddo whenever we can. It's a great way to serve up a frozen dessert that isn't the same old ice cream or sorbet.

ROASTED PEACH SEMIFREDDO WITH ALMOND BRITTLE

SERVES 8

PEACH SEMIFREDDO

10 ripe peaches, peeled, halved and stone removed

3 tablespoons honey

9 egg yolks

1½ cups sugar

¼ cup water

½ teaspoon vanilla paste

2½ cups heavy cream

ALMOND BRITTLE

1¼ cups sugar

10 tablespoons light corn syrup (or ½ cup plus 2 tablespoons)

½ cup water

1½ teaspoons kosher salt

2 tablespoons unsalted butter

1 cup almonds, lightly toasted and crushed

1½ teaspoons baking soda

PREPARE SEMIFREDDO

Preheat oven to 325°F. Place peaches cut side down in a large baking dish and drizzle with honey. Cover with foil and roast until peaches are soft, about 1 hour. Puree only enough peaches to yield 2 cups. Reserve remaining peaches for assembly.

Place yolks in the bowl of a mixer fitted with the paddle attachment and mix on high until pale and thick.

Combine sugar and water in a small saucepan and cook until mixture reaches 248°F. With mixer set on low, and working quickly, stream sugar syrup into egg yolks. Add vanilla paste, slightly increase mixer speed and continue mixing until no longer warm. Transfer to a large bowl.

In a separate bowl, beat cream until medium peaks form. Fold whipped cream into yolk mixture. Add peach puree and continue folding. Divide mixture evenly among eight 6-ounce ramekins and freeze for 4 to 6 hours, until firm.

PREPARE BRITTLE

Combine sugar, corn syrup, water and salt in a medium saucepan. Place over medium heat and stir until ingredients are dissolved. Increase heat to high and cook until temperature reaches 290°F. Add butter and almonds, and stir to combine. Continue cooking until temperature reaches 300°F. Add baking soda and stir for 30 seconds. Spread mixture evenly onto a Silpat-lined sheet pan. When hardened, use a food processor to grind brittle into small pieces. Store in an airtight container in a cool spot.

ASSEMBLE

Thinly slice reserved peaches and place on top of each ramekin. Sprinkle with almond brittle and serve.

This is like having breakfast at the end of your dinner, with the brioche *pain perdu* standing in for French toast and topped with everyone's favorite dish—ice cream.

BRIOCHE PAIN PERDU
WITH BLUEBERRIES AND LEMON ICE CREAM

SERVES 6 TO 8

BRIOCHE

2½ cups high-gluten bread flour
¼ cup sugar
1 tablespoon kosher salt
6 eggs
¼ ounce active dry yeast
12 ounces chilled high-fat butter, cut into small pieces
1 egg, beaten

LEMON ICE CREAM

4 cups heavy cream
2 cups milk
2½ tablespoons lemon zest
12 egg yolks
1½ cups sugar
1 teaspoon kosher salt
½ teaspoon vanilla paste

PREPARE BRIOCHE

Place flour, sugar and salt in the bowl of a stand mixer fitted with the dough hook and turn on low to combine.

In a saucepot, bring 2 inches of water to a simmer over medium heat. Place eggs and yeast in a large stainless steel bowl and whisk over simmering water until mixture is warm to the touch, making sure to whisk the entire time.

Pour warm egg mixture into mixing bowl and increase speed to medium. Mix until dough comes together and starts to form a ball.

With mixer running, add butter, piece by piece. Continue to mix until dough is shiny and makes a slapping sound in the bowl, about 10 minutes.

Place dough in a lightly buttered bowl and cover tightly with plastic wrap. Allow dough to proof at room temperature until it doubles in size (about 2 hours).

Uncover dough and knock down. Tightly cover again and place in refrigerator overnight.

On a floured surface, roll the cold dough into a log form.

Place dough in a lightly buttered pullman loaf pan and cover with plastic wrap. Allow to proof at room temperature until dough rises almost to the top of the pan (about 3 hours).

Preheat oven to 375°F.

Brush top of dough with beaten egg and bake for 30 to 35 minutes.

Remove from pan and allow to cool on a rack.

PREPARE ICE CREAM

Bring cream, milk and lemon zest to a simmer over medium heat. Remove from heat and allow to steep for 1 hour.

In a large mixing bowl, whisk yolks, sugar, salt and vanilla paste.

Bring cream mixture back to a simmer over medium heat and pour a quarter of the liquid into the egg yolks while whisking. Add another quarter of the hot liquid, still whisking, and then pour all back into the pot and place back on burner. Continue to cook at a low temperature, stirring with a wooden spoon until the mixture is thick and coats the back of the spoon. Place in a container and refrigerate overnight to allow to mature.

Strain mixture through a fine-mesh sieve. Place in an ice cream maker and freeze according to the machine manufacturer's directions.

»

BLUEBERRY COMPOTE

4 cups Florida blueberries

¾ cup sugar

2 tablespoons lemon juice

BRIOCHE PAIN PERDU

3 eggs

1 cup half-and-half

¼ teaspoon cinnamon

6 to 8 slices thick-cut brioche

3 tablespoons butter, divided

Kosher salt

PREPARE COMPOTE

Place 2 cups blueberries, sugar and lemon juice in a pot and cook over medium-high heat until berries are broken down and juices begin to thicken, about 8 minutes.

Remove from heat and stir in remaining blueberries. Set aside and allow to cool.

PREPARE PAIN PERDU

Whisk together eggs, half-and-half and cinnamon.

Place brioche slices in egg mixture, making sure to cover completely, and place on a wire rack for a moment to allow excess custard to drip off.

Melt 1 tablespoon butter in a sauté pan over medium heat.

Place 2 slices brioche in the pan and brown evenly on each side, about 2 minutes per side.

Remove from pan and repeat with remaining slices of brioche.

ASSEMBLE

Cut each slice of pain perdu into triangles and arrange on a plate, fanned out like a deck of cards.

Place a scoop of lemon ice cream on one side of the pain perdu.

Ladle about 3 tablespoons blueberry sauce over pain perdu and onto the plate.

We wanted to have some fun with devil's food cake and—voilà!—it wound up in a jar. The milk jam is really nothing more than condensed milk, which is cooked down. It's a big part of our dessert-pantry arsenal. What really seals the deal is when you top everything off with the panna cotta.

MILK CHOCOLATE PANNA COTTA

WITH MILK JAM AND DEVIL'S FOOD CAKE

SERVES 8

MILK JAM

1 (14-ounce) can sweetened condensed milk

DEVIL'S FOOD CAKE

2 eggs

1 cup plus 1 tablespoon sugar

1 teaspoon vanilla

¾ cup mayonnaise, preferably Duke's

1½ cups all-purpose flour

½ cup cocoa powder

¾ teaspoon baking soda

¼ teaspoon baking powder

½ teaspoon kosher salt

¾ cup water

MILK CHOCOLATE PANNA COTTA

2 cups heavy cream

1 cup sugar

½ vanilla bean, split and scraped

½ teaspoon kosher salt

9 ounces milk chocolate

3 ounces dark chocolate

6 sheets gelatin

4 cups half-and-half

»

PREPARE MILK JAM

Place the unopened can of condensed milk in a pot and cover with water. Bring to a gentle boil and leave for 1 hour. Using tongs, flip the can over and replenish water if necessary. Allow to gently boil for another hour.

Carefully remove can from water with tongs and allow to sit at room temperature for 10 to 15 minutes.

Place the can in an ice water bath to cool all the way through.

PREPARE DEVIL'S FOOD CAKE

Preheat oven to 350°F.

Beat eggs in a mixer on medium-high for 30 seconds. Add sugar gradually and beat until light and fluffy. Add vanilla and mayonnaise and beat to combine.

In a medium bowl, sift the dry ingredients together. Fold half the dry ingredients into the egg mixture. Add the water. Fold in remaining dry ingredients.

Prepare a half sheet pan with cooking spray and line with parchment paper. Pour batter into pan and use an offset spatula to spread batter into a thin, even layer.

Bake for 8 to 10 minutes, rotating pan halfway through, until a knife inserted into the center of the cake comes out clean.

Let cool and cut into 2½-inch rounds.

PREPARE PANNA COTTA

Place cream, sugar, vanilla bean (seeds and pod) and salt in a small saucepot and bring to a light simmer over medium-low heat, whisking to combine ingredients. Remove from heat.

Place both chocolates in a medium bowl. Place gelatin sheets in a separate bowl and cover with cold water, letting sit for at least 5 minutes.

Remove gelatin sheets from water and whisk into cream, making sure all the gelatin dissolves.

Strain hot cream mixture over chocolate and let sit for a few minutes, until chocolate melts.

Whisk half-and-half into chocolate mixture until smooth.

FOR ASSEMBLY

¼ cup sweetened condensed milk

CHEF'S TIP I like to take the scraps from the devil's food cake, crumble them and dry them in a low oven. I place the crumbles on top of the panna cotta and drizzle with a little olive oil and Maldon sea salt to serve.

ASSEMBLE

Spray eight 6-ounce jars or ramekins with cooking spray.

Place 1 tablespoon of room-temperature milk jam at the bottom of each jar. Place a cake round topside down into the milk jam, pushing down so the milk jam spreads to the sides of the jar. Spoon 1½ teaspoons sweetened condensed milk over cake round. Pour panna cotta mixture into jar until cake round is barely covered.

Repeat with remaining jars.

Place in refrigerator for 30 minutes or until panna cotta is set.

Remove from refrigerator and fill jars with more panna cotta mixture until jars are ¾ filled.

Return to refrigerator and allow to finish setting, at least 1 hour.

To serve, place each jar in a saucepot of water for 10 seconds to loosen the panna cotta from the jars. Turn each jar upside down on the center of a plate. (You may need to loosen the suction by gently pressing on one edge of the top of the panna cotta.)

ACKNOWLEDGMENTS

THE SCOPE OF A PROJECT LIKE THIS extends far beyond recipes and photos, and it's about much more than the person whose name is on the cover. This book would not have been possible without the help and commitment from my family, coworkers and friends.

I'm grateful to my family, for understanding that this is not a 9-to-5 career and for loving me regardless. Dad, thank you for teaching me "the harder I work, the luckier I get" (and how that also relates to fishing!). Mom, your confident push forward into this career set the tone for how I cook—always with love and with you on my shoulder. Thanks, too, for handpicking the person I admire most: my wife, Liz.

Elizabeth, your smile and soul give me true love. That love also allowed us to be fortunate enough to have two amazing children. Ryder and Ashby, your laughter and hugs carry me through the day, and the ability to see the world through your amazing eyes gives me unending happiness.

My partners at Luma on Park and Prato: Brian France, who encouraged me from the start that we should do this; and Austin Tate and Tim Noelke—a sincere thank you.

Bob Morris, of Story Farm: you convinced me that "now is the time" and agreed to go tarpon fishing with me under the assumption that if we could get along for two days in a boat, then we might be able to work together on a book. We didn't catch anything, but the book is finally done. Thanks, my friend.

Photographer Michael Pisarri: you perfectly captured our food though your lens. And your ability to make us laugh made every photo shoot enjoyable. We've known each other a long time, friend, and your talent never ceases to amaze me.

Most important, Derek Perez, chef of Luma, and Matthew Cargo, chef of Prato: you execute the conceptual vision nightly in my absence. Both of you have had a profound impact on my evolution as a chef. And to Brian Cernell, our talented and committed-to-the-core pastry chef: you complete the tripod of what keeps two separate kitchens intact and stable. I could not imagine working without you all. You are truly my brothers.

All of the sous chefs—Mike Tully, Vince Bink, Bryant Thorpe, Tim Lovero, Brandi Delhagen and Tiffany Jepson: your energy and enthusiasm keep the kitchens humming and productive. And Justin "Irish" Signor: without your assistance in recipe development, I would not be typing this page now.

All the players and smiling faces, from the hostesses, reservationists, waitstaff, stewards, busboys, food runners, chefs, prep teams and managers: you are the true foundation of it all, at Luma and Prato. Thank you for making our customers happy and well fed, and for keeping our restaurants profitable and popular.

Our little network of Florida farmers: Melanie and Roger of Waterkist, Denise of Rabbit Run, John and Amy of Frog Song, Charlie of Hammock Hollow, Dale of Lake Meadow Naturals, Henry of My Yard, Andy of Duda shrimp farm. Without you, we couldn't do our jobs. And to the awesome crew at Gary's Seafood, who keep the fish fresh and pick up from farmers as part of their statewide deliveries: thank you, thank you, thank you.

For all the chefs who tolerated me as a young cook: you taught me so much in so many different ways. Chef Anne Quatrano: you put the final grooming touches on me before I went out into the real world. Chef Drew Belline: I appreciate our daily ritual phone chats to talk about food and how much b.s. we are dealing with at any given moment (OK, and a few comments about how we could be fishing). These conversations are much-needed relief, for humor and for fueling a mutual inspiration in our fast-paced worlds of raising children and being chefs. (And they said we were bad for each other!) Chef Clayton Miller: we always pick up right where we left off, finishing each other's sentences and giving each other (hopefully) sound advice. And to Bob Amick, for always agreeing to disagree and for seeing above it all with laughter.

Brooks Emerson and Paul Collier: thank you both for always encouraging me to take a day off and go fishing! Our professional worlds are polar opposites, but when we join together under the sun, skimming the surface of glassy warm water on a hunt, fly rods in hand, we become a well-oiled fishing machine. Thank you both for sharing your Florida Everglades with me and helping me "slow down so I can speed up."

The entire Story Farm team—Ashley Fraxedas, Jason and Katie Farmand, David and Morgan Claytor: let's down some tequila right now. To our recipe testers—Minter Byrd, Pam Brandon, Victoria Allman, Susan Bourgoin—who made sure I was not crazy and all of this made some kind of sense: I think we should have some tequila too.

And to our friends and customers in Winter Park, your loyalty and support make this the perfect place to practice my craft and a great place to live.

PANTRY

CHICKEN STOCK
MAKES 4 QUARTS

1 whole chicken
1 gallon cold water
4 cups ice cubes
1 cup onion, thinly sliced
½ cup carrot, peeled and thinly sliced
½ cup celery, thinly sliced
2 garlic bulbs, halved crosswise
½ bunch fresh thyme sprigs
2 fresh bay leaves
2 tablespoons black peppercorns
¼ cup kosher salt

Remove skin and excess fat from chicken and rinse. Place in a large stockpot and add water. Simmer for 2 hours, constantly skimming the surface. Add ice, skim once more, and return to a simmer. Add remaining ingredients and simmer for additional 30 minutes. Strain slowly to prevent clouding of the stock.

PARMESAN STOCK
MAKES 8 CUPS

We use the inedible wax rinds of Parmigiano-Reggiano to extend flavor to our standard chicken stock. You can make this vegetarian by just using vegetable stock, but we love the body that the broth made from whole chickens gives this soup. We wrap the rinds in cheesecloth and tie with a string onto the pot handle to keep the rinds off the bottom of the pot while it simmers to prevent them from burning and scorching the stock. *Note: This broth makes one badass chicken noodle soup.*

1 pound Parmesan rinds, wrapped in cheesecloth with a string
9 cups Chicken Stock
4 bay leaves
2 tablespoons black peppercorns
2 garlic cloves, split in half

Tie the string to the side of a stockpot to elevate the rinds off of the bottom. Over medium heat, cover Parmesan with chicken stock, bay leaves, peppercorns and garlic. Skim fat as it comes to the surface. Simmer for 1 hour. Strain, discarding the solids and rinds.

SHELLFISH STOCK
MAKES 2 QUARTS

2 tablespoons grapeseed oil
1 pound shrimp shells (heads included) or blue crab shells
1 cup shallots, thinly sliced
¼ cup tomato paste
2 tablespoons black peppercorns
2 cups white wine
1 gallon water
4 tarragon sprigs
1 laurel bay leaf

In a large pot over medium-high heat, place oil and heat until dancing. Add shells and toast for 2 to 3 minutes, stirring constantly. Add shallots, tomato paste and black peppercorns. Cook for another 2 minutes. Deglaze with white wine and cook until almost dry. Cover with water, add tarragon and bay leaf, simmering for 20 minutes. Strain through a chinois. Place back on stove and reduce by half.

ROAST CHICKEN JUS
MAKES 1 QUART

This is a double stock. It uses a stock to moisten the roasted bones and then pull the roasted flavor and infuse it into the stock. As with any stock, it is very important to cook at a simmer (versus a rolling boil) and slightly offset the pot on the stove so the fat and impurities go to one side and can be easily skimmed off with a ladle. Our philosophy on stocks is that you can never skim them too much.

4 pounds chicken backs
2 fresh bay leaves
2 garlic bulbs, halved crosswise
½ bunch fresh thyme sprigs
2 tablespoons black peppercorns
½ cup tomato paste
6 quarts Chicken Stock, chilled

Preheat oven to 375°F. Place chicken backs on sheet pan in a single layer and roast until golden brown. Discard all accumulated fat.

Place roasted chicken, bay leaves, garlic, thyme, peppercorns and tomato paste in a large stockpot.

Pour stock over ingredients and simmer for 6 to 8 hours, skimming constantly.

Strain through a fine chinois and place liquid back into a clean stockpot. Bring to a simmer and reduce to approximately 1 quart.

VEAL JUS

MAKES 4½ QUARTS

7 pounds veal bones (can substitute beef bones)
2 calves feet, split
4 pounds onions, whole, divided
2 pounds carrots, whole, divided
2 pounds celery, whole, divided
12 garlic cloves, divided
2 cups tomato paste, divided
1 pound parsley sprigs, divided
¼ pound thyme sprigs, divided
½ cup black peppercorns, divided
14 fresh bay leaves, divided

In a 400°F oven, roast and lightly brown the veal bones.

Place calves feet in a pot, cover with water and simmer for 2 minutes. Remove and rinse with cold water.

Place the roasted veal bones and the calves feet in a large stock pot and cover with water. Simmer for 2 hours, constantly skimming impurities from the surface.

Add half of all remaining ingredients and continue to simmer and skim for another 6 hours. Using a fine chinois, strain liquid. Place liquid in a separate container from bones and vegetables, and refrigerate both overnight.

The next day, remove reserved liquid from refrigerator and set aside. Place cooked bones and vegetables in a large stockpot. Add remaining ingredients and cover with water. Simmer for 4 hours, skimming fat as needed. Strain liquid, discarding bones and vegetables. Let liquid come to room temperature and combine with reserved liquid.

SOFFRITO CRUDO

MAKES 2 CUPS

Soffrito Crudo and Glazed Soffrito (below) are essential ingredients in our kitchen. They provide the backbone for many of our dishes.

1 cup yellow onion, brunoise

½ cup celery, brunoise

½ cup carrot, brunoise

Combine all ingredients and set aside to use as needed.

GLAZED SOFFRITO

MAKES 1 CUP

1 tablespoon unsalted butter

2 tablespoons water

Pinch of kosher salt

Small pinch of sugar

Soffrito Crudo (above)

Place butter, water, salt and sugar in a saucepan just large enough to hold vegetables in a single layer. Turn heat to low and add soffrito crudo. Cover with a cartouche and bring to a simmer. When water begins to evaporate, remove cover and stir once. Replace cartouche and continue to cook until vegetables are 90 percent done. Place in single layer on a parchment-lined sheet pan and refrigerate until cool.

COMPOUND BUTTER (FOR PIPING)

¼ pound unsalted butter, room temperature

1 garlic clove, Microplaned

1 tablespoon tarragon, chopped

1 tablespoon chives, chopped

1 tablespoon parsley, chopped

¼ teaspoon kosher salt

8 turns of a black pepper grinder (preferably Tellicherry, as it is the most fragrant and well-rounded)

Mix all ingredients well and place in a piping bag. Keep at room temperature until needed.

SHERRY VINAIGRETTE

MAKES ABOUT 2 CUPS

2 tablespoons shallots

⅓ cup sherry vinegar (Xérès origin preferred)

2 tablespoons Dijon-style mustard

1¼ cups extra-virgin olive oil

Kosher salt and freshly ground black pepper

In a small bowl, cover shallots and mustard with vinegar. Let soak for 20 minutes. Whisk in olive oil and season to taste.

*** RED WINE VINAIGRETTE**

Substitute red wine for sherry vinegar

WHITE PICKLING LIQUID

MAKES ENOUGH LIQUID TO FILL 9 (1-QUART) JARS WITH VEGETABLES

1 cup white wine vinegar

½ cup water

½ cup sugar

1 tablespoon kosher salt

Spices as desired

Place first 4 ingredients in a saucepan and simmer. Add spices. Immediately remove from heat. If using as a hot pickle liquid, pour over vegetables. Otherwise, follow standard pickling instructions.

*** RED PICKLING LIQUID**

Replace white wine vinegar with red wine vinegar

PICKLED RAMPS

1 pound ramps, white part only, cleaned and bulb removed

2 cups Red Pickling Liquid

Bring pickling liquid to a simmer and add ramps. Cook for 2 minutes. Cool and store in airtight container in refrigerator. Keeps forever and a day!

PICKLING MARINADE (A.K.A. CONSERVA OR AGRODOLCE)

MAKES 4 CUPS

4 cups extra-virgin olive oil

2 cups shallots, thinly sliced

¼ cup garlic cloves, thinly sliced

1 tablespoon kosher salt

¼ teaspoon sugar

¼ cup vinegar (can change from red, white, balsamic, sherry pending use)

2 tablespoons thyme, chopped

½ tablespoon tarragon, whole

Heat ¼ cup oil in a saucepan over medium-high heat. Sweat the shallots, garlic, salt and sugar until soft, about 5 minutes. Add the vinegar and cook until most of the liquid has evaporated. Cover with rremaining oil and add thyme and tarragon. Remove from heat immediately.

EGGPLANT AGRODOLCE

MAKES 3 CUPS

In this sublime recipe that is used daily in both of our kitchens, the eggplants are blanched in a traditional pickling liquid (versus salted water), then submerged in a flavorful oil marinade. Matt Cargo, chef de cuisine of Prato, introduced this unique technique to me when I presented him with forty pounds of heirloom eggplant from Rabbit Run Farm.

2½ cups Japanese or heirloom eggplant, halved and sliced ⅛ inch thick

2½ cups White Wine Pickling Liquid

1 cup extra-virgin olive oil

¼ cup shallots, sliced paper thin

2 tablespoons garlic cloves, sliced paper thin

1 teaspoon crushed red pepper

1 tablespoon parsley, chopped

1 tablespoon tarragon, chopped

1 teaspoon thyme leaves, chopped

Kosher salt

Heat oil over low heat to 180°F. Add shallots, garlic and crushed pepper. Steep for 3 minutes and avoid browning; set aside. Heat pickling liquid in a separate saucepot and bring to a boil. Submerge eggplant for 1 minute or until tender. Remove eggplant from liquid and place in aromatic olive oil. Fold in fresh herbs and salt to taste. Refrigerate in an airtight container for up to 2 weeks.

BASIL AIOLI

MAKES 2 CUPS

3 ounces basil leaves (about 2 to 3 cups, loosely packed)

2 egg yolks

1 tablespoon Dijon mustard

2 garlic cloves, Microplaned

3 tablespoons lemon juice

¾ cup plus 1 tablespoon extra-virgin olive oil

¾ cup plus 1 tablespoon grapeseed oil

½ cup basil puree

Kosher salt

Blanch basil leaves in boiling water for 30 seconds. Drain, reserving blanching liquid, and place basil in an ice bath to retain its vibrant color.

Cool blanching liquid. Squeeze basil dry. Place basil in blender with 3 tablespoons blanching liquid and puree until smooth. Keep cold.

In a small bowl, whisk eggs, mustard, pinch of salt, garlic and lemon juice. In a separate bowl, combine oils. While whisking egg mixture constantly in the same direction, slowly drizzle in the oil. After mixtures have come together, fold in the basil puree. Keep cold until needed.

BASIL OIL

4 cups basil leaves, packed

¾ cup extra-virgin olive oil, chilled

Bring a gallon of heavily salted water to a simmer. Blanch basil leaves for 20 to 30 seconds and then transfer to a bowl of ice water. Drain basil, gently squeezing out excess water. Place in a chilled blender and add olive oil. Puree for 1 minute, slightly heating the oil but being careful to not get it hot. Place puree in a metal bowl placed over another bowl filled with ice. Stir to quickly chill and retain bright color. Refrigerate for 12 to 24 hours. Puree mixture once again until warm but not hot. Place in three layers of cheesecloth and tie ends with a string. Hang in refrigerator overnight to allow the oil to drip out of the puree. Can be made ahead and frozen.

CHORIZO OIL

(Must be made a day in advance)

2 ounces shallot (about 1 large), thinly sliced

1 ounce garlic (about 3 cloves), peeled and halved

8 ounces dried chorizo, diced

¼ cup tomato paste

1 bay leaf

1 teaspoon spicy smoked pimentón (Spanish paprika)

1 tablespoon sweet smoked pimentón

2⅔ cups grapeseed oil

Lightly sweat shallot and garlic for a couple of minutes over medium-high heat. Add chorizo, and increase heat slightly to let chorizo release its fat. Cook for about 10 minutes.

Add tomato paste, bay leaf and both pimentóns. Cook until very fragrant, stirring frequently so mixture does not stick.

Add oil and bring to a simmer. Remove from heat, place in a sealed container and refrigerate overnight.

The next day, put chorizo oil in a saucepot and return to a simmer. Cook for 2 minutes and strain though a fine chinois. Chill oil until ready to use, discarding chorizo sediment.

TOMATO WATER

YIELDS 3 CUPS

1½ pounds tomatoes, very ripe
2 tablespoons kosher salt
¼ teaspoon sugar
4 basil leaves

Place all ingredients in blender and puree until smooth.

Line a colander with a damp cheesecloth, folded over twice. Place a bowl under the colander to catch juices. Pour puree into colander, place in refrigerator overnight and discard cheesecloth in the morning. Keep tomato water chilled until needed.

BASIC BRINE

1 gallon (4 quarts) water, divided
1 cup sugar
1 cup kosher salt
10 black peppercorns
1 garlic clove, split
Sage bundle
Various spices as desired

Before starting, make sure you have 3 quarts ice water on hand. In large pot, bring 1 quart water to boil with all spices. Simmer for 3 minutes. Remove from heat. Add ice water.

PANGRATTATO

(Must be made 1 to 2 days in advance)

2 slices bread, diced in ½-inch cubes and dried for 1–2 days in warm spot
3 garlic cloves, Microplaned
1 tablespoon plus 1 teaspoon extra-virgin olive oil
Kosher salt to taste

Let garlic marinate in oil for 2 hours, then strain, discarding garlic. In blender, pulse bread until it resembles cornmeal. Place breadcrumbs in sauté pan over medium-high heat and add oil to coat. Constantly move the pan to toast evenly for 4 to 5 minutes. When breadcrumbs are golden brown, season and cool on a paper-lined plate. Can keep for 5 days.

PREMIUM PASTA BLEND

2½ cups 00 flour
1 cup plus 1 tablespoon semolina flour

Mix together in a small bowl and use per pasta recipe instructions.

STANDARD BREADING PROCEDURE

1 cup all-purpose flour
2 large eggs, beaten
1 cup panko "fino"

Place ingredients side by side in separate bowls. Dip ingredient to be fried in flour, then eggs, then panko before cooking.

JERRY GARCIA SPICE BLEND

2 tablespoons cumin seeds
2 tablespoons coriander seeds
1 tablespoon fennel seed
2 tablespoons black peppercorns
½ cup kosher salt
1 tablespoon cayenne pepper
2 tablespoons Spanish paprika

Combine first 4 ingredients and place in a small frying pan. Toast until fragrant and a light smoke begins to appear. Cool on a parchment-lined sheet pan. Grind the cooled spices and mix with salt, cayenne and paprika.

GANDHI SPICE BLEND

1 tablespoon sweet curry powder
½ teaspoon crushed red pepper
2 tablespoons fennel seed
2 tablespoons coriander seed
1 tablespoon cumin seed
1 tablespoon brown mustard seeds
1 tablespoon yellow mustard seeds
1 cinnamon stick, cracked into 4 pieces

Combine all spices in a blender or coffee grinder and pulse into a lightly textured powder. Store in an airtight container.

SOURCES

Anson Mills
Grits, polenta
www.ansonmills.com

Baldor Specialty Foods
Molino Spadoni flour
www.baldorfood.com

Cedar Creek Shellfish
Mosquito Lagoon clams
www.cedarcreekshellfish.com

Cortez Bottarga
Bottarga (cured Florida mullet roe)
www.cortezbottarga.com

D'Artagnan
Chestnuts, truffles, foie gras
www.dartagnan.com

Fante's Kitchen Shop
Pasta-making tools
www.fantes.com

Fresh & Wild
Mushrooms
www.freshwild.com

Frog Song Organics
Seasonal vegetables
www.frogsongorganics.com

Gary's Seafood
Fresh Florida fish, stone crabs, sea urchin, specialty products (Ativa, transglutamine)
www.garyseafood.com

La Quercia
Cured meats: lardo, prosciutto, pancetta, guanciale
www.laquercia.us

Lake Meadow Naturals
Eggs, poultry
www.lakemeadownaturals.net

Mote Caviar
Florida sturgeon caviar
www.motecaviar.com

My Yard Farm
Squash blossoms, seasonal vegetables
www.myyardfarm.com

Palmetto Creek
Pork
www.bestpork.us

Penzeys Spices
Spices, herbs, seasonings
www.penzeys.com

Rabbit Run Farm
Heirloom vegetables, strawberries, tropical fruits
www.rabbitrunfarmllc.com

Seely's Ark
Rabbit
352.489.8353

Steve & Mike Shellfish Co.
Uni
www.smshellfish.com

Waterkist Farm
Tomatoes, microgreens
407.322.7110

INDEX

Numbers in **bold** indicate pages with photos